Collins

11+
Maths

Quick Practice Tests
Ages 9-10

Faisal Nasim

Contents

ACKNOWLEDGEMENTS

The author and publisher are grateful to the copyright holders for permission to use quoted materials and images.

All images are © HarperCollins*Publishers* Limited

Every effort has been made to trace copyright holders and obtain their permission for the use of copyright material. The author and publisher will gladly receive information enabling them to rectify any error or omission in subsequent editions. All facts are correct at time of going to press.

Published by Collins

An imprint of HarperCollins*Publishers* Limited

1 London Bridge Street

London SE1 9GF

HarperCollins*Publishers*

Macken House, 39/40 Mayor Street Upper,

Dublin 1, D01 C9W8, Ireland

ISBN: 9781844198900

First published 2017

This edition published 2020

Previously published as Letts

10 9 8 7 6

© HarperCollins*Publishers* Limited 2020

All rights reserved. No part of this publication may be reproduced, stored in a retrieval system, or transmitted, in any form or by any means, electronic, mechanical, photocopying, recording or otherwise, without the prior permission of Collins.

British Library Cataloguing in Publication Data.

A CIP record of this book is available from the British Library.

Author: Faisal Nasim

Commissioning Editor: Michelle I'Anson

Editor and Project Manager: Sonia Dawkins

Cover Design: Kevin Robbins

Text Design, Layout and Artwork: Q2A Media

Production: Paul Harding

Printed in Great Britain by Ashford Colour Ltd

MIX
Paper
FSC™ C007454
www.fsc.org

Please note that Collins is not associated with CEM in any way. This book does not contain any official questions and it is not endorsed by CEM.

Our question types are based on those set by CEM, but we cannot guarantee that your child's actual 11+ exam will contain the same question types or format as this book.

About this book

Familiarisation with 11+ test-style questions is a critical step in preparing your child for the 11+ selection tests. This book gives children lots of opportunities to test themselves in short, manageable bursts, helping to build confidence and improve the chance of test success.

It contains 45 tests designed to build key numeracy skills.

- Each test is designed to be completed within a short amount of time. Frequent, short bursts of revision are found to be more productive than lengthier sessions.

- CEM tests often consist of a series of shorter, time-pressured sections so these practice tests will help your child become accustomed to this style of questioning.

- If your child does not complete any of the tests in the allocated time, they may need further practice in that area.

- We recommend your child uses a pencil to complete the tests, so that they can rub out the answers and try again at a later date if necessary.

- Children will need a pencil and a rubber to complete the tests and some spare paper for rough working. They will also need to be able to see a clock/watch and should have a quiet place in which to do the tests.

- Your child should **not** use a calculator for any of these tests.

- Answers to every question are provided at the back of the book, with explanations given where appropriate.

- After completing the tests, children should revisit their weaker areas and attempt to improve their scores and timings for those tests.

Download a free progress chart, maths glossary and topic checklist from our website
collins.co.uk/11plus

Test 1

Draw a line in the box below the correct answer.

EXAMPLE

Round 764 to the nearest 10.

760	750	770	790
⊏═══⊐	⊏⊐	⊏⊐	⊏⊐

---

(1) Calculate 3,423 + 723

4,473	4,146	2,700	4,991
⊏⊐	⊏⊐	⊏⊐	⊏⊐

(2) Calculate 6,471 ÷ 9

719	711	722	678
⊏⊐	⊏⊐	⊏⊐	⊏⊐

(3) Which of the following expresses the figure three million, two hundred and seventeen thousand and one in digits?

3,217,001	3,217,101	3,217,100	3,217,010
⊏⊐	⊏⊐	⊏⊐	⊏⊐

(4) What is the next number in this sequence?

6,550   6,575   6,600   6,625   6,650   ?

6,680	6,650	6,625	6,675
⊏⊐	⊏⊐	⊏⊐	⊏⊐

(5) The temperature in the morning is 12°C. In the afternoon, the temperature rises by 5°C.

At night, the temperature then decreases by 19°C.

What is the temperature at night?

32°C	−2°C	37°C	2°C
⊏⊐	⊏⊐	⊏⊐	⊏⊐

6 Ben bought 2 apples from a shop and paid with a £10 note.

An apple costs 34 p.

How much change did Ben receive?

£0·64

£9·32

£9·36

£9·66

7 What is the order of rotational symmetry of this shape?

0

2

4

6

8 $\frac{1}{3}X = 27$

What is the value of X?

3

9

27

81

9 What is the sum of the prime numbers in the grid below?

34	23	65
22	1	18
14	51	44
6	38	17

40

91

92

41

10 What is $\frac{33}{9}$ as a mixed number?

$7\frac{2}{9}$

$3\frac{7}{9}$

$4\frac{6}{9}$

$3\frac{2}{3}$

Test 2

You have 3 minutes to complete this test.

You have 5 questions to complete within the given time.

Use the diagram below to help you answer the questions in this test. Write the correct answer in the boxes provided (one digit per box).

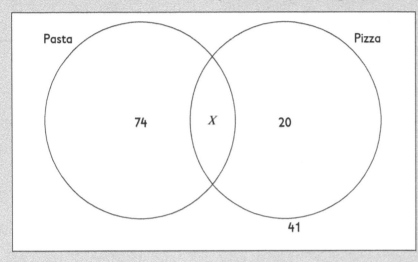

This Venn diagram shows the results of a survey about the food liked by a group of children.

1. How many children like pasta but not pizza?

2. How many children like neither pizza nor pasta?

3. If 150 children were surveyed, how many like both pizza and pasta?

4. What fraction of the 150 children only like pizza?
   Write your answer as a fraction in its lowest terms.

5. $\frac{2}{7}$ of the children who like pizza also like fish and chips.

   How many of the children like pizza but not fish and chips?

Score: .... / 5

Test 3

Write the correct answer in the boxes provided (one digit per box).

EXAMPLE

How much greater is 34 grams than 21 grams?

[1] [3] g

---

1 The coordinates of 3 corners of a square are (4, 0),
(4, 4) and (0, 4).

What are the coordinates of the 4th corner?

([ ] , [ ])

2 How many sevenths are there in 21?

[ ] [ ] [ ]

3 Bill waters his plants on the 1st January and then continues to
do so on alternate days for the rest of the month.

How many times does Bill water his plants in January?

[ ] [ ]

4 Write the number 54·67892 to 2 decimal places.

[ ] [ ] · [ ] [ ]

5 Calculate $(7 \times 8) - (8 \times 7) + (8 + 7)$

[ ] [ ]

6 How many millimetres are there in 1·2 m?

[ ] , [ ] [ ] [ ] mm

7 Rebecca bought 3 plates for £39.

What is the cost of 7 plates?

£ [ ] [ ]

8 Bob scored a total of 54 marks in 2 tests.
He then scored 30 marks in his 3rd test.

What was Bob's average score for the 3 tests?

[ ] [ ]

9 Robert is 136 cm tall. Henry is $\frac{3}{4}$ the height of Robert.
Sam is 20 cm shorter than Robert.

What is the range of their heights?

[ ] [ ] cm

Score: .... / 9

7

Test 4

You have 4 minutes to complete this test.

You have 8 questions to complete within the given time.

Circle the letter below the correct answer.

EXAMPLE

Round 676 to the nearest 10.

680	670	675	690
Ⓐ	B	C	D

(1) The base of a triangle measures 7 cm and its height measures 8 cm. What is twice the area of the triangle?

112 cm²	56 cm²	28 cm²	15 cm²
A	B	C	D

(2) What is the sum of all the sevens in the grid below?

3	5	2	7	8	1	3	2	0	9
1	3	4	6	0	9	1	3	4	5
7	8	2	0	8	9	1	4	5	7
2	6	8	1	6	1	0	3	0	5
3	2	8	4	5	9	7	6	5	6
6	1	4	1	5	4	3	6	7	9
7	5	7	2	6	8	7	3	8	0
6	6	4	2	0	0	9	2	8	7
9	7	5	4	5	9	4	0	9	3
2	3	8	1	9	0	1	4	2	8

70	10	12	63
A	B	C	D

(3) How many two-digit square numbers are there?

1	6	4	7
A	B	C	D

(4) Tim has £120 in his bank account. He spends $\frac{1}{3}$ of it on a game and £20 on a meal.

What percentage of Tim's money remains in his bank account?

50%	66%	20%	75%
A	B	C	D

(5) 25% of the children in School A have brown hair.

30% of the children in School A have black hair.

The remaining 225 children have blonde hair.

How many children are there in School A?

500	450	300	225
A	B	C	D

(6) 7 out of every 9 football players are right-footed.

98 football players attend a football tournament.

Which of the following is the best estimate of the number of right-footed players at the tournament?

55	45	91	76
A	B	C	D

(7) A, B and C are 3 points plotted on a straight line in alphabetical order.

The distance between A and B is three times the distance between B and C.

If the distance between A and C is 24 cm, what is the distance between B and C?

18 cm	20 cm	6 cm	12 cm
A	B	C	D

(8) Figure 1 is made from identical hexagons.

Each hexagon has a perimeter of 42 cm.

What is the perimeter of Figure 1?

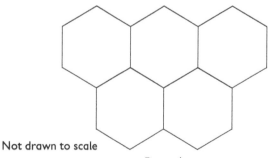

Not drawn to scale

Figure 1

84 cm	98 cm	72 cm	112 cm
A	B	C	D

Score: .... / 8

9

Test 5

You have 5 minutes to complete this test.

You have 10 questions to complete within the given time.

Draw a line in the box below the correct answer.

EXAMPLE

Round 764 to the nearest 10.

760	750	770	790

---

1 How many different factors does the number 9 have?

1	9	3	2

2 Calculate the quotient of 108 and 3.

36	324	111	105

3 $\frac{3}{8} = \frac{24}{X}$

What is the value of X?

48	128	72	64

4 The area of a square is 16 cm².

What is the perimeter of the square?

4 cm	16 cm	32 cm	64 cm

5 Anna, Sarah and Kate shared some prize money between them.

Anna received twice as much as Kate. Sarah received half as much as Anna.

What ratio shows how much Anna, Sarah and Kate received, respectively?

2:1:2	1:1:1	1:2:1	2:1:1

6 7 pencils each measure 12 cm.

If the pencils were laid end to end, what is the combined length of the pencils, in metres?

0·84 m	8·4 m	0·12 m	84 m
⬭	⬭	⬭	⬭

7 Ellen rolls a fair die.

What is the probability that she rolls a 3?

$\dfrac{1}{2}$	$\dfrac{2}{6}$	$\dfrac{1}{6}$	$\dfrac{3}{6}$
⬭	⬭	⬭	⬭

8 There are 9 goldfish. Each goldfish eats 3 g of fish food per day.

How much fish food in total do the 9 goldfish eat per week?

3 g	27 g	21 g	189 g
⬭	⬭	⬭	⬭

9 The clock below shows the time in Delhi in the afternoon.

The time in London is $6\dfrac{1}{2}$ hours behind the time in Delhi.

What is the current time in London?

23:41	10:41	23:11	11:11
⬭	⬭	⬭	⬭

10 An art gallery sells paintings for £12·50.

A current offer discounts the purchase of a second painting by 50% when 2 are bought together.

What is the cost of 2 paintings?

£12·50	£6·25	£25·00	£18·75
⬭	⬭	⬭	⬭

Score: .... / 10

Test 6

You have **3** minutes to complete this test.

You have **5** questions to complete within the given time.

Use the diagrams below to help you answer the questions in this test. **Write the correct answer in the boxes provided (one digit per box).**

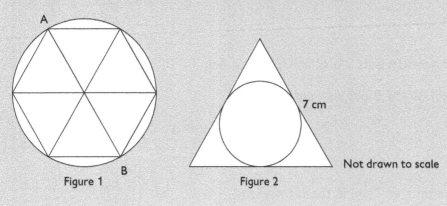

Figure 1

Figure 2

7 cm

Not drawn to scale

---

(1) Figure 1 consists of a circle with a hexagon inscribed inside it.

The hexagon is formed from 6 identical equilateral triangles.

If the length of AB is 13 cm, what is the perimeter of 1 of these triangles?

⬜⬜.⬜ cm

(2) Figure 2 consists of a circle inscribed inside an equilateral triangle.

What is the order of rotational symmetry of Figure 2?

⬜

(3) What is the perimeter of Figure 2?

⬜⬜ cm

(4) Aziz draws a pentagon. The perimeter of the pentagon is 10% greater than the perimeter of the hexagon in Figure 1.

What is the perimeter of the pentagon?

⬜⬜.⬜ cm

(5) An ant walks around the full perimeter of Figure 2 at a speed of 2 cm/second.

How long does it take the ant to walk around the perimeter of Figure 2?

Round your answer to the nearest whole number.

⬜⬜ seconds

Score: .... / 5

Test 7

Write the correct answer in the boxes provided (one digit per box).

EXAMPLE

How much greater is 34 grams than 21 grams? | 1 | 3 | g

---

(1) Calculate 3,240 ÷ 9

(2) Calculate 5 ÷ 0·5

(3) What is the next number in this sequence?

4, 5, 9, 14, 23, ?

(4) 20% of the 200 lizards on an island are yellow.

$\frac{1}{4}$ of the remaining lizards are black.

What percentage of the lizards on the island are
neither yellow nor black? %

(5) Which whole number is less than half of 34 but greater than $\frac{1}{3}$ of 45?

(6) A monthly internet bill is £34.

How much is paid annually for the internet? £

(7) Jill's scores for 4 tests are 12, 3, 9 and G. Her average score is 6.

What is the value of G?

(8) Milk bottles cost £1·50 each.

Rafael buys a dozen milk bottles and receives a 20% discount.

How much does Rafael save? £ .

Score: .... / 8

13

Test 8

You have 5 minutes to complete this test.

You have 10 questions to complete within the given time.

Circle the letter below the correct answer.

Round 676 to the nearest 10.

680	670	675	690	650
(A)	B	C	D	E

---

1 Which number has a value less than 3?

$\frac{19}{6}$	$\frac{14}{5}$	$\frac{21}{7}$	$\frac{30}{9}$	$\frac{40}{4}$
A	B	C	D	E

2 Rachel takes the 6:21 a.m. train from Cardiff. The train leaves on time but arrives 21 minutes late. The train arrives at 9:30 a.m.

How long would the train journey have taken if it was not late?

3 h 9 min	3 h 1 min	2 h 48 min	2 h 45 min	2 h 7 min
A	B	C	D	E

3 Every 4th person that enters a museum has brown hair.

Every 5th person that enters the museum wears glasses.

If 100 people enter the museum, how many of them have brown hair and wear glasses?

5	6	8	10	7
A	B	C	D	E

4 $70 < X < 80$

X divided by 7 has a remainder of 1.

Which of these could be the value of X?

74	77	79	72	78
A	B	C	D	E

5 How many right angles are there within Figure 1?

Figure 1

4	5	6	7	8
A	B	C	D	E

6 Martin bought 2 pencils and 3 pens. He paid with a £5 note and received £3·70 in change.

If a pen costs 30 p, what is the cost of a pencil?

£1·30	£0·30	£0·45	£0·20	£0·35
A	B	C	D	E

7 What is 1 less than $2(4^2)$?

31	16	32	63	65
A	B	C	D	E

8 The area of a grey circle is twice the area of a white circle.

Figure 2 consists of the white circle placed on top of the grey circle.

What percentage of Figure 2 is grey?

Figure 2

65%	33%	25%	50%	29%
A	B	C	D	E

9 Marco hands out some sweets to his friends. Each friend receives 7 sweets and Marco has 4 sweets left over.

Which of the following could be the original number of sweets that Marco had?

53	45	38	28	17
A	B	C	D	E

10 4 sides of a pentagon are 3·5 cm, 2·2 cm, 1·9 cm and 6·7 cm.

If the pentagon has a perimeter of 17 cm, what is the length of the 5th side?

2·9 cm	3·1 cm	2·6 cm	3·8 cm	2·7 cm
A	B	C	D	E

Score: .... / 10

Test 9

You have 5 minutes to complete this test.

You have 10 questions to complete within the given time.

Draw a line in the box below the correct answer.

EXAMPLE

Round 764 to the nearest 10.

760   750   770   790

(1) Rectangles B and G have the same perimeter.

What is the value of X?

Rectangle G   6 cm

11 cm

Not drawn to scale

Rectangle B   13 cm

X cm

13 cm   6 cm   8 cm   4 cm

(2) What is $\frac{9}{6}$ expressed as a decimal?

1·6   9·6   1·5   6·9

(3) 8 apples cost 88 p.

How much do 12 apples cost?

£0·11   £0·88   £1·32   £1·21

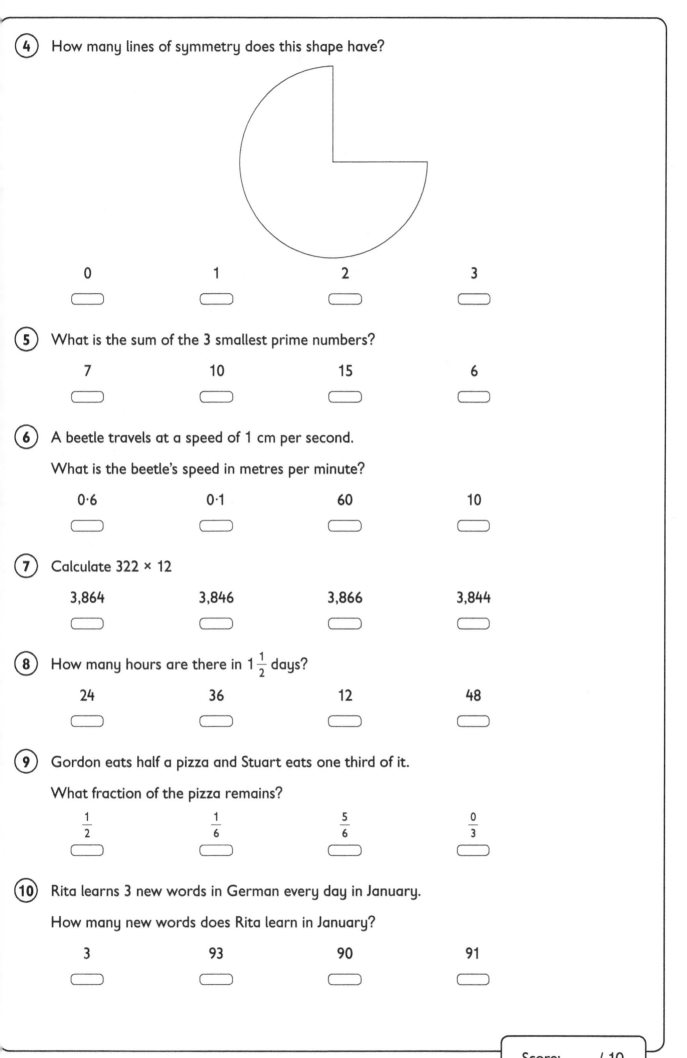

4 How many lines of symmetry does this shape have?

0	1	2	3
⬭	⬭	⬭	⬭

5 What is the sum of the 3 smallest prime numbers?

7	10	15	6
⬭	⬭	⬭	⬭

6 A beetle travels at a speed of 1 cm per second.

What is the beetle's speed in metres per minute?

0·6	0·1	60	10
⬭	⬭	⬭	⬭

7 Calculate 322 × 12

3,864	3,846	3,866	3,844
⬭	⬭	⬭	⬭

8 How many hours are there in $1\frac{1}{2}$ days?

24	36	12	48
⬭	⬭	⬭	⬭

9 Gordon eats half a pizza and Stuart eats one third of it.

What fraction of the pizza remains?

$\frac{1}{2}$	$\frac{1}{6}$	$\frac{5}{6}$	$\frac{0}{3}$
⬭	⬭	⬭	⬭

10 Rita learns 3 new words in German every day in January.

How many new words does Rita learn in January?

3	93	90	91
⬭	⬭	⬭	⬭

Score: .... / 10

Test 10

You have 3 minutes to complete this test.

You have 5 questions to complete within the given time.

Use the clocks below to help you answer the questions in this test. Write the correct answer in the boxes provided (one digit per box).

Clock 1

Clock 2

Clock 1 shows the time Jill left her house in the afternoon and Clock 2 shows the time she returned home later in the day.

(1) For how long was Jill away from home?

☐ h ☐☐ min

(2) Jill arrived at the library 74 minutes after she left her home.

At what time did Jill arrive at the library?

Write your answer in 24-hour clock format.

☐☐ : ☐☐

(3) Jill went to bed $3\frac{1}{5}$ hours after she arrived home.

At what time did Jill go to bed?

Write your answer in 24-hour clock format.

☐☐ : ☐☐

(4) Jill woke up at 07:34.

For how many hours was Jill asleep?

☐☐ h ☐☐ min

(5) What is the angle formed between the hour and minute hand in Clock 2?

☐☐☐ °

Score: .... / 5

Test 11

Write the correct answer in the boxes provided (one digit per box).

EXAMPLE

How much greater is 34 grams than 21 grams?   [1] [3] g

(1) What is the mode of the following numbers?

34, 32, 31, 37, 34, 39, 35, 36, 38

(2) What is half of the perimeter of a regular octagon with sides of 7·5 cm?   cm

(3) Calculate $(1 + 3)^2 + 1^2 + 3^2$

(4) How many five-pence coins are needed to make £1·45?

(5) A running track is 400 m long.

Ethan runs around the track $3\frac{1}{2}$ times.

How far does Ethan run?   ☐·☐ km

(6) A bag contains 9 pieces of paper each with a unique whole number between 2 and 10.

A piece of paper is picked at random.

What is the probability that the paper is numbered 7?

(7) Write $\frac{14}{5}$ as a decimal.   ☐·☐

(8) Calculate $100 \times 4·56 \times 0·1$ ☐☐·☐

(9) The price of a box of vegetables increases from £8 to £14.

What percentage increase is this?   ☐☐ %

(10) What is twice the sum of 2 angles in an equilateral triangle?   ☐☐☐°

Score: .... / 10

19

Test 12

You have 5 minutes to complete this test.

You have 10 questions to complete within the given time.

Circle the letter below the correct answer.

1 How many factors does the number 100 have?

7	8	6	9
A	B	C	D

2 How much liquid is in the container below?

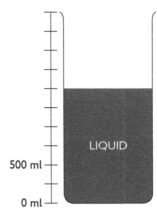

750 ml	1·5 l	2 l	1,000 ml
A	B	C	D

3 2 angles in a scalene triangle are 74° and 81°.

What is the size of the 3rd angle in the triangle?

50°	81°	25°	23°
A	B	C	D

(4) A piece of wood measures 2 m 24 cm. It is cut into 4 equal pieces.

What is the total length of 3 of the pieces?

56 cm	112 cm	150 cm	168 cm
A	B	C	D

(5) Which ratio is equivalent to 65:45?

11:10	9:5	13:9	12:9
A	B	C	D

(6) What is the order of rotational symmetry for this shape?

0	1	2	3
A	B	C	D

(7) What number is missing from this sequence?

1·01   0·97   ?   0·89   0·85

0·96	0·93	0·91	0·81
A	B	C	D

(8) The lights in an office are turned on for $\frac{7}{12}$ of a whole day.

How many hours are the lights turned on for?

12 hours	10 hours	7 hours	14 hours
A	B	C	D

(9) A cardigan is sold with a 10% discount. The original price was £11·10.

What is the sale price of the cardigan?

£9·99	£10·11	£1·11	£9·90
A	B	C	D

(10) The weight of a stone is 2·56 kg, rounded to 2 decimal places.

What is the maximum possible weight of the stone in grams?

2,566 g	2,565 g	2,564 g	2,555 g
A	B	C	D

Score: .... / 10

Test 13

You have 5 minutes to complete this test.

You have 10 questions to complete within the given time.

Draw a line in the box below the correct answer.

EXAMPLE

Round 764 to the nearest 10.

760	750	770	790
⎯	⬭	⬭	⬭

---

(1) Calculate 6,101 − 5,009

1,001	1,092	1,088	1,011
⬭	⬭	⬭	⬭

(2) What is the missing digit in this sum?

$$
\begin{array}{r}
\square\,1\ 7 \\
+\quad 3\ 5\ 8 \\
\hline
1,1\ 7\ 5 \\
\end{array}
$$

5	6	7	8
⬭	⬭	⬭	⬭

(3) $AB = 44$

$A - B = 7$

What is the value of A?

4	7	11	15
⬭	⬭	⬭	⬭

(4) Rob buys a piece of string that is 1 m 34 cm in length.

He cuts off 8 pieces from the string, each measuring 6 cm.

How long is the string now?

128 cm	102 cm	86 cm	96 cm
⬭	⬭	⬭	⬭

5 What fraction of 2 weeks is 2 days?

$\frac{1}{7}$ ⬭ $\frac{3}{14}$ ⬭ $\frac{1}{6}$ ⬭ $\frac{1}{10}$ ⬭

6 Train A leaves Town B at 15:23. It arrives at Town C after 3 hours and 21 minutes.

At what time does Train A arrive at Town C?

15:41 ⬭ 12:02 ⬭ 18:44 ⬭ 15:09 ⬭

7 What is the value of the missing term in this sequence?

33, ?, 38, 47, 63, 88

34 ⬭ 35 ⬭ 37 ⬭ 36 ⬭

8 Figure 1 is made from 20 blocks, each with a side length of 1 cm.

How many more blocks must be added to Figure 1 to create a cube with side length of 4 cm?

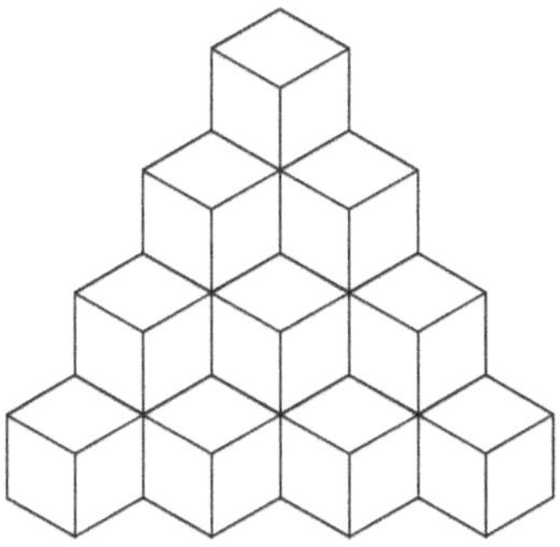

Not drawn to scale

Figure 1

20 ⬭ 64 ⬭ 52 ⬭ 44 ⬭

9 Which of these values is the smallest?

| 0·45 | $\frac{4}{10}$ | 0·423 | $\frac{4}{20}$ |

0·45 ⬭ $\frac{4}{10}$ ⬭ 0·423 ⬭ $\frac{4}{20}$ ⬭

10 John takes 3 tests and his average score is 95%.

His average score on the first 2 tests is 94%.

What did John score on the 3rd test?

94% ⬭ 95% ⬭ 96% ⬭ 97% ⬭

Score: .... / 10

23

Test 14

You have 3 minutes to complete this test.

You have 5 questions to complete within the given time.

Use the table below to help you answer the questions in this test. **Write the correct answer in the boxes provided (one digit per box) or draw a line in the box below the correct answer.**

	Date of birth
Adam	12th August
Simon	16th August
Ted	11th July
Fred	19th July

The table above shows the birth dates of 4 boys who were all born in the same year.

---

1 Which boy is the second oldest?

Adam   Simon   Ted   Fred

⟨ ⟩   ⟨ ⟩   ⟨ ⟩   ⟨ ⟩

2 How many days separate the birth dates of Ted and Adam?

3 This year, Ted's birthday is on a Tuesday.

On what day is Fred's birthday this year?

Sunday   Tuesday   Friday   Wednesday

⟨ ⟩   ⟨ ⟩   ⟨ ⟩   ⟨ ⟩

4 Adam's sister is 2 years, 3 months and 5 days older than him.

On what date is Adam's sister's birthday?

19th   7th   12th   29th

⟨ ⟩   ⟨ ⟩   ⟨ ⟩   ⟨ ⟩

5 What fraction of the months in the year have 30 days?

Write your answer as a fraction in its lowest terms.

Score: .... / 5

24

Test 15

Write the correct answer in the boxes provided (one digit per box).

EXAMPLE

How much greater is 34 grams than 21 grams?

| 1 | 3 | g

---

(1) Calculate 15% of 6,000

(2) The sum of 3 angles in a quadrilateral is 234°.

What is the size of the 4th angle?

(3) 2 faces of a cube are painted red.

What fraction of the cube's surface area is red?

Write your answer as a fraction in its lowest terms.

(4) What is the sum of the 2 greatest prime numbers less than 20?

(5) How many lines of symmetry does an isosceles triangle have?

(6) 6 eggs cost the same as 9 bananas.

If an egg costs 18 p, what is the cost of 2 bananas?

p

(7) What digit is in the hundredths column in 2,345·2857?

(8) Calculate 50% of 20% of 18

Score: .... / 8

Test 16

You have 5 minutes to complete this test.

You have 10 questions to complete within the given time.

Circle the letter below the correct answer.

EXAMPLE

Round 676 to the nearest 10.

680	670	675	690	650
(A)	B	C	D	E

(1) What is the product of 325 and 25?

8,300	7,500	8,315	8,225	8,125
A	B	C	D	E

(2) At 5 a.m. the temperature of a liquid is −3°C. The temperature of the liquid rises by 3°C per hour until 6 p.m.

What is the temperature of the liquid at 6 p.m.?

29°C	36°C	27°C	39°C	22°C
A	B	C	D	E

(3) Bella has £4·20 and Ella has $\frac{1}{4}$ as much money as Bella.

How much money do they have altogether?

£4·20	£1·05	£3·15	£5·25	£2·05
A	B	C	D	E

(4) Figure 1 was formed by removing a square with a width of 1 cm from each corner of a square with a width of 5 cm.

What is the perimeter of Figure 1?

Not drawn to scale

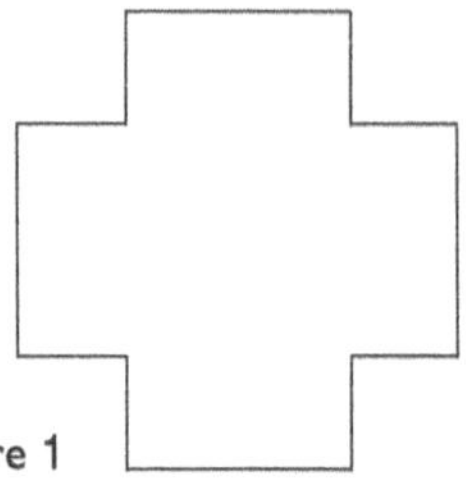

Figure 1

16 cm	25 cm	21 cm	20 cm	14 cm
A	B	C	D	E

5 The table on the right shows the number of burgers sold per day in a restaurant for 1 week.

If 22 burgers are sold per day on average in this week, how many burgers were sold on Tuesday?

Day	Burgers
Monday	19
Tuesday	
Wednesday	23
Thursday	21
Friday	22
Saturday	24
Sunday	18

24	27	22	23	19
A	B	C	D	E

6 What fraction of these numbers are prime?

78, 45, 32, 44, 63, 1, 13

$\frac{1}{7}$	$\frac{2}{7}$	$\frac{3}{7}$	$\frac{5}{7}$	$\frac{2}{5}$
A	B	C	D	E

7 A car travels at a speed of 40 km per hour.

How far does the car travel in 15 minutes?

30 km	20 km	10 km	15 km	13 km
A	B	C	D	E

8 7 out of every 10 visitors to a museum are adults.

Adult tickets costs £5.

What is the total cost of adult tickets for 30 visitors?

£110	£135	£150	£95	£105
A	B	C	D	E

9 A special plant cell divides itself into 3 new special plant cells every hour.

If there is 1 special cell at 11 a.m., how many will there be at 2 p.m.?

1	27	12	36	110
A	B	C	D	E

10 What value does the 7 represent in 235,750?

7,000	700	7	70	70,000
A	B	C	D	E

Score: .... / 10

Test 17

You have 5 minutes to complete this test.

You have 10 questions to complete within the given time.

Draw a line in the box below the correct answer.

EXAMPLE

Round 764 to the nearest 10.

760	750	770	790
⬭̶	⬭	⬭	⬭

---

(1) Which of these fractions is the greatest?

$\frac{2}{6}$	$\frac{1}{8}$	$\frac{3}{9}$	$\frac{1}{2}$
⬭	⬭	⬭	⬭

(2) Figure 1 is an equilateral triangle with sides of 9 cm.

How many equilateral triangles with sides of 3 cm can fit into Figure 1?

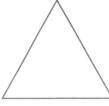

Not drawn to scale

Figure 1

1	5	9	13
⬭	⬭	⬭	⬭

(3) Every day, a rabbit eats 2 more carrots than the day before.

If the rabbit eats 9 carrots on day 1, how many does it eat on day 6?

21	15	19	18
⬭	⬭	⬭	⬭

(4) $70,000 \times 1,500 = 105,000,000$

$(105,000,000 \div 70,000) \div 2 = A$

What is the value of A?

1,000	105,000	750	1,500
⬭	⬭	⬭	⬭

(5) ✦ is a function.

$A✦ = 3A + 45$

What is the value of $3✦$?

| 36 | 49 | 54 | 21 |
| ⬭ | ⬭ | ⬭ | ⬭ |

(6) The lengths of 2 sides of a triangle are 6 cm and 4 cm.

Which of the following cannot be the length of the 3rd side?

| 3 cm | 5 cm | 2 cm | 6 cm |
| ⬭ | ⬭ | ⬭ | ⬭ |

(7) $\frac{1}{2} \times \frac{1}{2} \times \frac{1}{2} \times 440 = S$

What is the value of S?

| 55 | 110 | 220 | 400 |
| ⬭ | ⬭ | ⬭ | ⬭ |

(8) What is the sum of the even numbers from the list of numbers in the box below?

| 33, 49, 90, 55, 91, 18, 11, 97, 51, 64, 59 |

| 82 | 172 | 154 | 118 |
| ⬭ | ⬭ | ⬭ | ⬭ |

(9) Figure 2 is a parallelogram.

What is the value of $G°$?

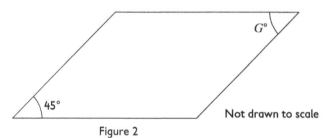

45°

Not drawn to scale

Figure 2

| 45° | 180° | 55° | 135° |
| ⬭ | ⬭ | ⬭ | ⬭ |

(10) 3 apples and 4 oranges cost £2·50.

2 apples and 4 oranges cost £2·20.

What is the cost of 1 orange?

| 40 p | 30 p | 45 p | 50 p |
| ⬭ | ⬭ | ⬭ | ⬭ |

Test 18

Use the number cards below to help you answer the questions in this test. Write the correct answer in the boxes provided (one digit per box).

4	3	9	9	1

(1) What fraction of the number cards show prime numbers?

☐
─
☐

(2) What is the largest number that can be made by rearranging 4 of the number cards?

☐ , ☐ ☐ ☐

(3) Subtract the smallest number that can be made by rearranging all the number cards, from the largest number that can be made by rearranging all the number cards.

☐ ☐ , ☐ ☐ ☐

(4) Divide the sum of the number cards by 5.

Write your answer as a decimal.

☐ . ☐

(5) What is the quotient of the sum of the 2 largest number cards and the product of the 2 smallest number cards?

☐

Test 19

You have 4 minutes to complete this test.

You have 8 questions to complete within the given time.

Write the correct answer in the boxes provided (one digit per box).

EXAMPLE

How much greater is 34 grams than 21 grams? $\boxed{1}\boxed{3}$ g

---

1. A train passes through Station A every 7 minutes.

   A train passes through Station A at 14:00.

   How many more trains will pass through before 15:00? $\boxed{}$

2. A plane flies at an altitude of 8,000 m. It then descends by 2,000 m.

   What is the percentage decrease in the plane's altitude? $\boxed{}\boxed{}$ %

3. In 2015 £1 had the same value as $1·50.

   In 2015 what was the value in pounds of $9? £$\boxed{}$·$\boxed{}\boxed{}$

4. A triangle with an area of 12 cm² is placed on a square with an area of 36 cm².

   What fraction of the square is not covered by the triangle?

   Write your answer as a fraction in its lowest terms. $\dfrac{\boxed{}}{\boxed{}}$

5. A map has a scale of 1:100,000.

   What is the actual distance represented by 2 cm on the map? $\boxed{}$ km

6. What is the product of the number of right angles in a square and the number of right angles in an equilateral triangle? $\boxed{}$

7. A container holds 22 tins.

   How many containers are needed to hold 89 tins? $\boxed{}$

8. 7 nails are needed to secure 1 painting to a wall.

   How many nails are needed to secure 77 paintings? $\boxed{}\boxed{}\boxed{}$

Score: .... / 8

31

Test 20

Circle the letter below the correct answer.

EXAMPLE

Round 676 to the nearest 10.

680	670	675	690
(A)	B	C	D

1 There are 74 rows of passenger seats in an aeroplane.

Each row has 6 seats except 2 rows which have 5 seats.

How many passenger seats are there in the aeroplane?

74	442	370	444
A	B	C	D

2 A rectangle has a width of 7 cm and a perimeter of 44 cm.

What is the length of the rectangle?

14 cm	30 cm	15 cm	44 cm
A	B	C	D

3 A regular hexagon has a perimeter of 42 cm.

What is the perimeter of a regular octagon that has the same side length as this hexagon?

42 cm	64 cm	56 cm	49 cm
A	B	C	D

4 Artem has 4 coins in his pocket: 10 p, 2 p, 50 p and 20 p.

He picks 1 coin out of his pocket at random.

What is the probability that the coin has an odd value?

$\frac{1}{2}$	$\frac{1}{4}$	$\frac{3}{4}$	0
A	B	C	D

5 Which of these numbers has the largest value?

5·6	$5\frac{7}{10}$	$\frac{35}{7}$	$\frac{18}{3}$
A	**B**	**C**	**D**

6 What is the value of $R°$?

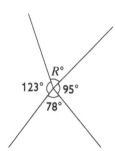

123° 95° R° 78°

Not drawn to scale

59°	64°	93°	74°
A	**B**	**C**	**D**

7 What measurement is shown by the arrow?

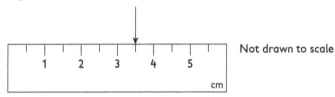

Not drawn to scale

3·5 m	35 cm	0·35 cm	35 mm
A	**B**	**C**	**D**

8 The sum of 3 consecutive numbers is 18.

What is the product of the 3 numbers?

90	120	210	336
A	**B**	**C**	**D**

9 In a survey, 35% of the respondents said they enjoyed gardening.

60% of the respondents said they did not enjoy gardening.

The remainder were unsure.

If 1,000 people took part in the survey, how many were not sure whether they enjoyed gardening?

50	40	500	5
A	**B**	**C**	**D**

10 What is the value of $3(3·3 - 2·7) + 4$?

5·8	4·6	1·8	5·5
A	**B**	**C**	**D**

Score: .... / 10

Test 21

Draw a line in the box below the correct answer.

EXAMPLE

Round 764 to the nearest 10.

760	750	770	790
⸺	⬭	⬭	⬭

① Calculate 2·345 − 3·245

0·9	1·1	−0·9	0·845
⬭	⬭	⬭	⬭

② A notebook weighs 76 g.

How much less than 1 kg is the combined weight of 7 notebooks?

0·486 kg	0·468 kg	0·532 kg	0·924 kg
⬭	⬭	⬭	⬭

③ A five-cent coin has a diameter of 7 mm.

45 cents worth of five-cent coins are placed end to end in a line.

What is the length of this line?

3·5 cm	4·9 cm	6·3 cm	2·5 cm
⬭	⬭	⬭	⬭

④ The diagram below represents a field at a scale of 1:100.

What is the area of the actual field?

9 cm

Not drawn to scale

4 cm

3·6 m²	36 m²	360 m²	3,600 m²
⬭	⬭	⬭	⬭

(5) A triangle has an area of 42 cm² and a height of 7 cm.

What does the base of the triangle measure?

6 cm	12 cm	8 cm	24 cm
⬭	⬭	⬭	⬭

(6) A pizza is cut into 12 equal slices.

What is the value of angle $r°$?

Not drawn to scale

36°	35°	40°	30°
⬭	⬭	⬭	⬭

(7) Monkey 1 and Monkey 2 share 81 peanuts in a ratio of 2:1.

What fraction of the peanuts does Monkey 1 receive?

$\frac{1}{3}$	$\frac{2}{3}$	$\frac{2}{1}$	$\frac{1}{2}$
⬭	⬭	⬭	⬭

(8) $84C = 81C$

What is the value of C?

81	0	7	12
⬭	⬭	⬭	⬭

(9) 3 years ago, Rahul was 7 years old and his father was 5 times his age.

How old will Rahul's father be in 2 years' time?

35	37	40	43
⬭	⬭	⬭	⬭

(10) How much greater is the product of 7 and 8 than the sum of 7 and 8?

8	41	15	56
⬭	⬭	⬭	⬭

Score: .... / 10

Test 22

You have 3 minutes to complete this test.

You have 5 questions to complete within the given time.

Use the diagram below to help you answer the questions in this test. Write the correct answer in the boxes provided (one digit per box) or draw a line in the box below the correct answer.

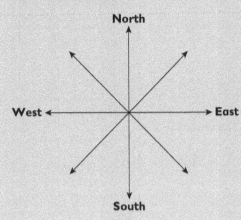

1. Malik faces north and turns 45° anticlockwise.

   In which direction does Malik now face?

   northwest   southeast   east   northeast

2. What is the bearing of north from east? ☐☐☐°

3. Mark walks 5 m east, 7 m north and 5 m west.

   How far is Mark from his starting point? ☐ m

4. Dimitry faces northeast and makes 3 right angle turns clockwise.

   In which direction is Dimitry now facing?

   northwest   southeast   east   southwest

5. Maddy faces east and turns 135° clockwise.

   What fraction of a full turn does Maddy make?

   Write your answer as a fraction in its lowest terms.

Score: .... / 5

Test 23

You have 4 minutes to complete this test.

You have 8 questions to complete within the given time.

Write the correct answer in the boxes provided (one digit per box).

EXAMPLE

How much greater is 34 grams than 21 grams?　　　　　1 3 g

1. Without overlapping, how many squares with a side length of 4 cm can fit into a rectangle with a width of 16 cm and a length of 20 cm?

2. Robert took 3 tests and his average score was 32.

   What was Robert's combined score on the 3 tests?

3. Calculate 2·24 m − 111 cm　　　cm

4. Apples cost 45 p and pears cost 25 p.

   What is the total cost of 11 apples and 4 pears?　£ ⃞ · ⃞ ⃞

5. The length of 4 sides of a pentagon are 4·5 cm, 2 cm, 5 cm and 2·5 cm. The perimeter of the pentagon is 15 cm.

   What is the length of the 5th side of the pentagon?　cm

6. A film is 90 minutes long. It is shown in a cinema which has a 15 minute interval halfway through the film.

   If the film begins at 15:40, at what time does the interval begin?　⃞⃞ : ⃞⃞

7. How many more sides does a heptagon have than a triangle?

8. What is the greatest prime factor of 35?

Score: .... / 8

37

Test 24

You have 5 minutes to complete this test.

You have 10 questions to complete within the given time.

Circle the letter below the correct answer.

Round 676 to the nearest 10.

680	670	675	690	650
(A)	B	C	D	E

1. Calculate 4·743 + 47·43

51·473	52·173	474·43	52·137	51·748
A	B	C	D	E

2. 30 squirrels in a park are red. This represents 25% of the total number of squirrels in the park.

   How many squirrels in the park are not red?

30	25	120	80	90
A	B	C	D	E

3. What is the difference between the largest and smallest factors of the number 4,000?

2,400	3,999	1,998	456	4,000
A	B	C	D	E

4. What is the difference in seconds between $\frac{1}{5}$ of an hour and $\frac{1}{6}$ of an hour?

60 seconds	90 seconds	120 seconds	150 seconds	45 seconds
A	B	C	D	E

5. 9 boxes of oranges cost £63.

   Each box contains 35 oranges.

   What is the cost of 1 orange?

20 p	2 p	35 p	70 p	12 p
A	B	C	D	E

(6) Wendy walks 1·5 km every morning and 1·5 km every evening.

How far does Wendy walk in 1 week?

10·5 km	21 km	3 km	15 km	11 km
A	B	C	D	E

(7) Figure 1 consists of a triangle placed above a rectangle.

The area of the triangle is 10·5 cm².

The area of Figure 1 is 52·5 cm².

What is the value of X?

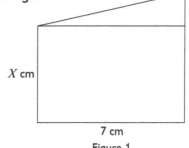

X cm

7 cm

Figure 1

Not drawn to scale

6	4	8	9	7
A	B	C	D	E

(8) Square A has an area of 16 cm².

The length of each side of the square is increased by 25% to create Square B.

What is the perimeter of Square B?

20 cm	25 cm	16 cm	12 cm	10 cm
A	B	C	D	E

(9) 2 angles in a triangle are 55° and 70°.

What type of triangle is this?

right angled	scalene	isosceles	equilateral	parallel
A	B	C	D	E

(10) The clock to the right shows the time Bob wakes up in the morning.

He goes to bed 15 hours and 34 minutes later.

At what time does Bob go to bed?

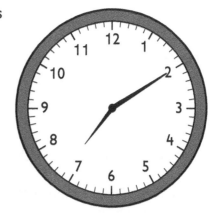

15:34	20:34	21:36	19:54	22:44
A	B	C	D	E

Score: .... / 10

Test 25

Draw a line in the box below the correct answer.

EXAMPLE

Round 764 to the nearest 10.

760	750	770	790
⊑══⊒	⊂▢⊃	⊂▢⊃	⊂▢⊃

---

(1) Tim has £15. He buys 2 drinks for £1·30 each and a packet of crisps for 99 p.

How much money does Tim have left?

£13·70	£11·41	£3·59	£12·71
⊂▢⊃	⊂▢⊃	⊂▢⊃	⊂▢⊃

(2) Rectangle A has a width of 5 cm and a length of 7 cm.

Rectangle B has dimensions that are twice as large as Rectangle A.

What is the area of Rectangle B?

35 cm²	70 cm²	140 cm²	100 cm²
⊂▢⊃	⊂▢⊃	⊂▢⊃	⊂▢⊃

(3) What is the product of the 3 consecutive numbers that have a sum of 15?

15	60	90	120
⊂▢⊃	⊂▢⊃	⊂▢⊃	⊂▢⊃

(4) What fraction of 2 hours is 12 minutes?

$\frac{2}{12}$	$\frac{1}{3}$	$\frac{1}{5}$	$\frac{1}{10}$
⊂▢⊃	⊂▢⊃	⊂▢⊃	⊂▢⊃

(5) What is the range of the values in the box below?

> 3·11 m, 20 mm, 3·5 cm, 97 mm, 411 cm, 4·01 m

399 cm	440 mm	4·09 m	303 cm
⊂▢⊃	⊂▢⊃	⊂▢⊃	⊂▢⊃

6 The pie chart below shows the results of a survey asking 420 students about their favourite food.

How many students chose 'Chips' as their favourite food?

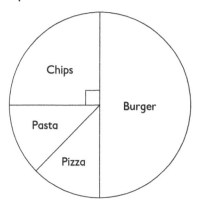

90	220	105	100
⬭	⬭	⬭	⬭

7 Gina decides to wear a hat and a belt with her outfit. She has 3 hats and 4 belts.

How many different combinations of hat and belt can Gina choose from?

3	4	12	24
⬭	⬭	⬭	⬭

8 Which of these values is the smallest?

$\frac{4}{5}$	0·82	$\frac{7}{20}$	0·81
⬭	⬭	⬭	⬭

9 The timetable below shows the schedule of 2 trains.

How much longer does it take Train B than Train A to travel from Frochester to Gochester?

	Train A	Train B
Frochester	17:34	19:21
Bochester	17:49	19:40
Gochester	18:03	19:59
Lochester	18:11	20:08

12 minutes	9 minutes	8 minutes	10 minutes
⬭	⬭	⬭	⬭

10 A watch is fast and gains 2 minutes per hour.

If this watch currently shows a time of 15:39, what time will it show in 2 hours?

17:39	17:35	17:43	17:41
⬭	⬭	⬭	⬭

Score: .... / 10

Test 26

You have 3 minutes to complete this test.

You have 5 questions to complete within the given time.

Use the diagrams below to help you answer the questions in this test. Write the correct answer in the boxes provided (one digit per box).

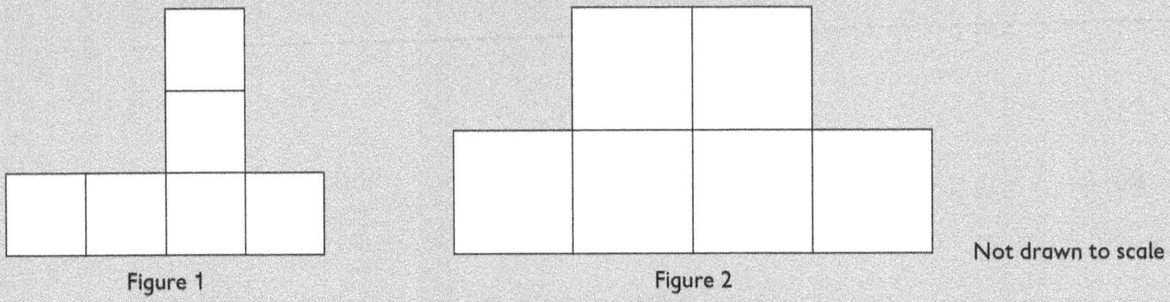

Figure 1

Figure 2

Not drawn to scale

Figure 1 is formed from identical squares, each with an area of 16 cm².

Figure 2 is formed from identical squares, each with an area of 25 cm².

1. What is the area of Figure 2? ☐☐☐ cm²

2. What is the perimeter of Figure 1? ☐☐ cm

3. The squares in Figure 1 are painted red and blue in the ratio 1:2.

   What fraction of the squares are painted blue? ☐/☐

4. How many lines of symmetry does Figure 1 have? ☐

5. Pattern A is made using 6 identical copies of Figure 1.

   What is the area of Pattern A? ☐☐☐ cm²

Score: .... / 5

Test 27

You have 4 minutes to complete this test.

You have 7 questions to complete within the given time.

Write the correct answer in the boxes provided (one digit per box).

EXAMPLE

How much greater is 34 grams than 21 grams? | 1 | 3 | g

1. Ben has a mean score of 12 after 3 tests.

   Ben takes a 4th test and his mean increases by 1.

   What was Ben's 4th test score?

2. Zoe had 30 p consisting of an equal number of one-pence and two-pence coins.

   How many coins did Zoe have altogether?

3. 11 lemons cost £7·70.

   What is the cost of 13 lemons?   £ ☐ · ☐ ☐

4. Jane had a total of 25 books. 10 of them were blue and the rest were red.

   What percentage of Jane's books were red?   ☐ ☐ %

5. $\frac{17}{34} = \frac{4}{V}$

   What is the value of V?

6. Write 7·5% as a decimal number.   ☐ · ☐ ☐ ☐

7. Lorries have 6 wheels and cars have 4 wheels.

   A car park contains 20 cars and 5 lorries.

   What is the total number of wheels in the car park?

Score: .... / 7

43

Test 28

You have 5 minutes to complete this test.

You have 10 questions to complete within the given time.

Circle the letter below the correct answer.

EXAMPLE

Round 676 to the nearest 10.

680	670	675	690
Ⓐ	B	C	D

(1) How many even whole numbers are greater than 18 but less than 31?

5	6	7	8
A	B	C	D

(2) What is the value of angle $b°$?

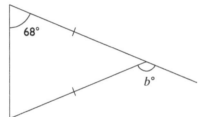

68°

$b°$

Not drawn to scale

25°	44°	68°	136°
A	B	C	D

(3) The roots of a tree grow by half a metre each year.

If the roots are currently 3·25 m long, how many years will it take until they are 7·75 m long?

4	5	8	9
A	B	C	D

(4) Gerald prepares a meal for his 8 friends and himself.

He wishes to serve 200 g of meat per person.

How much meat must Gerald prepare?

1·6 kg	0·2 kg	1·8 kg	3·2 kg
A	B	C	D

5 Rob, Rachel and Rick share £3 in the ratio 1:3:1.

What percentage of the money does Rick receive?

30%	20%	10%	35%
A	B	C	D

6 A sequence is created with the nth term $2n + 1$.

What is the sum of the 3rd and 5th terms in the sequence?

7	8	18	11
A	B	C	D

7 The length of 1 side of a regular octagon is $(2X - 2)$ long.

Which expression shows the perimeter of the octagon?

$16X - 16$	$2X - 2$	$16X - 8$	$16X + 16$
A	B	C	D

8 This diagram contains small and large black circles.

Not drawn to scale

The area of each small black circle is 1·5 cm².

The area of each large black circle is 2·5 cm².

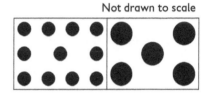

What is the combined area of all the black circles?

16·5 cm²	4 cm²	29 cm²	12·5 cm²
A	B	C	D

9 A trough contains 7 litres of water.

9 pigs each drink 250 ml of water per hour from the trough.

How much water is left in the trough after 3 hours?

6·75 litres	4·75 litres	2·25 litres	0·25 litres
A	B	C	D

10 What is the difference between the largest and smallest number below?

323, 233, 333, 332, 223

110	101	100	99
A	B	C	D

Score: .... / 10

45

Test 29

Draw a line in the box below the correct answer.

EXAMPLE

Round 764 to the nearest 10.

760	750	770	790

---

1 How many times greater than 12 is 84?

72	7	64	8

2 Calculate 674 + 43 + 234 − 233

718	720	719	699

3 Ellie has 6 coins in her pocket that have a total value of 27 p.

5 of the coins have the same value.

What is the value of the other coin?

1 p	2 p	5 p	10 p

4 756 × 698 = 527,688

Calculate 0·756 × 69·8

52·7688	527·688	5276·88	52768·8

5 Harry has 240 marbles. He gives away $\frac{1}{4}$ of them. $\frac{1}{3}$ of the remaining marbles are green.

How many of the remaining marbles are not green?

60	120	90	180

(6) A car takes 20 minutes to travel 13 km.

What is the car's speed in kilometres per hour (kph)?

24 kph	26 kph	20 kph	39 kph
⬭	⬭	⬭	⬭

(7) Figure 1 is a regular pentagon. How many lines of symmetry does Figure 1 have?

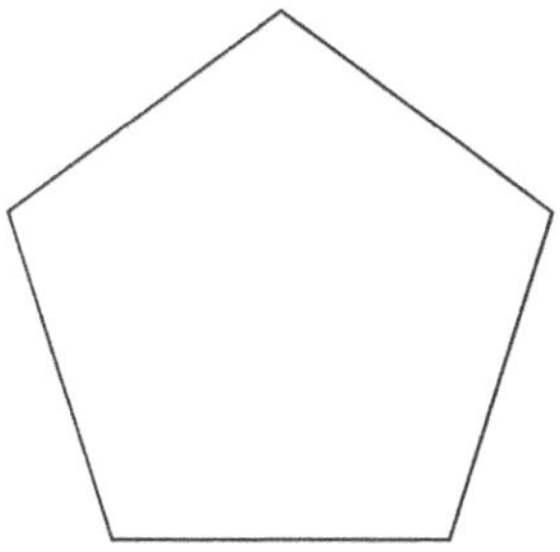

Figure 1

0	1	4	5
⬭	⬭	⬭	⬭

(8) Shape A is made from identical squares, each with a perimeter of 16 cm.

What is the perimeter of Shape A?

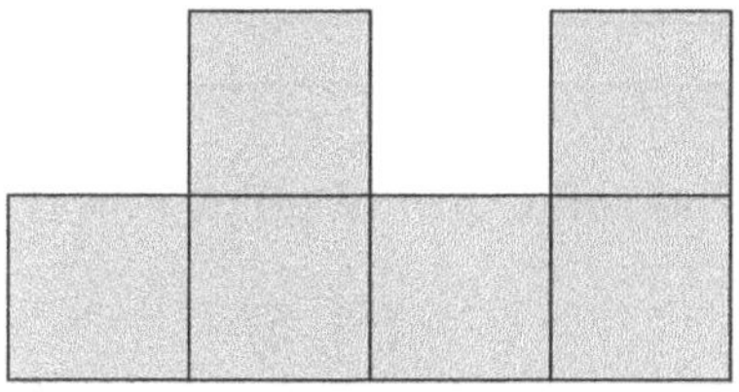

Not drawn to scale

Shape A

64 cm	14 cm	56 cm	60 cm
⬭	⬭	⬭	⬭

(9) What decimal fraction is 1 cm of 1 km?

0·00001	0·001	0·0001	0·0101
⬭	⬭	⬭	⬭

(10) Bill and Jen each earn £8 per hour at work.

If they both worked from 9 a.m. to 5:30 p.m. on Wednesday, how much did they earn in total?

£68	£72	£17	£136
⬭	⬭	⬭	⬭

Score: .... / 10

Test 30

You have 3 minutes to complete this test.

You have 5 questions to complete within the given time.

Use the grid below to help you answer the questions in this test. Write the correct answer in the boxes provided (one digit per box) or draw a line in the box below the correct answer.

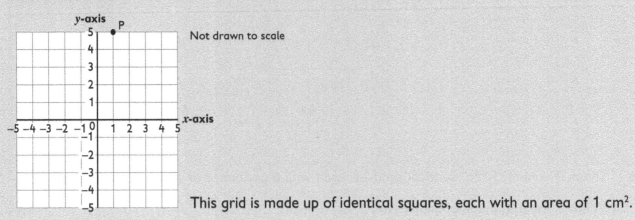

Not drawn to scale

This grid is made up of identical squares, each with an area of 1 cm².

---

1 What are the coordinates of the reflection of point P in the *y*-axis?

(1, −5) (−1, −5) (−1, 5) (1, 5)

⊂⊃ ⊂⊃ ⊂⊃ ⊂⊃

2 What are the coordinates of the reflection of point P in the *x*-axis?

(1, −5) (−1, −5) (−1, 5) (1, 5)

⊂⊃ ⊂⊃ ⊂⊃ ⊂⊃

3 The coordinates of point B are (1, 0).

The coordinates of point H are (3, 0).

What is the area of the triangle PBH? ☐ cm²

4 The diagonally opposite vertices of a rectangle have coordinates (−2, 1) and (−4, 4).

What is the area of this rectangle? ☐ cm²

5 Point F is 5 cm south and 4 cm west of point P.

What are the coordinates of point F? (-☐,☐)

Score: .... / 5

Test 31

Write the correct answer in the boxes provided (one digit per box).

EXAMPLE

How much greater is 34 grams than 21 grams?

| 1 | 3 | g

1. Which of the following is a multiple of 4?

   13, 38, 34, 48

   ☐ ☐

2. Vic is three times older than George.

   Last year, George was 8 years old.

   How old will Vic be next year?

   ☐ ☐

3. Sophia had 25 p. She spent $\frac{2}{5}$ of it and lost 7 p.

   How much money does Sophia have left?

   £ ☐ . ☐ ☐

4. Subtract the value of the 7 in 3,472 from the value of the 3 in 2,319.

   ☐ ☐ ☐

5. How many lines of symmetry does a regular octagon have?

   ☐

6. The 5 terms in a sequence are x, $2x$, $4x$, $6x$, $8x$.

   If the 3rd term in the sequence is 60, what is the 4th term?

   ☐ ☐

7. The coordinates of point A are (4, 0) and the coordinates of point B are (4, 8).

   What are the coordinates of the mid-point of the line AB?

   (☐ , ☐)

8. A milk bottle can hold 75 ml of milk.

   How many bottles are needed to hold half a litre?

   ☐

Score: .... / 8

49

Test 32

You have 5 minutes to complete this test.

You have 9 questions to complete within the given time.

Circle the letter below the correct answer.

EXAMPLE

Round 676 to the nearest 10.

680	670	675	690	650
(A)	B	C	D	E

1 $17 + 2 - 8 + 21 = G \times 2$

What is the value of G?

15	2	10	16	14
A	B	C	D	E

2 Mohammed works at a petrol station for 3 hours every day from 27th June to 10th July inclusive.

Mohammed gets paid £9 per hour.

How much is Mohammed paid for his work in total?

£27	£324	£378	£351	£444
A	B	C	D	E

3 Betty finishes a race in 7th place, ahead of 17 other competitors.

Apart from Betty, how many people took part in the race?

23	16	17	24	15
A	B	C	D	E

4 Ian and Helen had the same number of marbles. Ian then gave Helen 17 of his marbles.

Helen now has twice as many marbles as Ian.

How many marbles do they have altogether?

44	34	88	97	102
A	B	C	D	E

(5) What is the remainder when 75,643 is divided by 7?

6	3	1	4	5
A	B	C	D	E

(6) Figure 1 is made from identical cubes.

How many cubes are used to construct Figure 1?

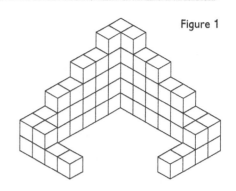

Figure 1

54	50	55	59	51
A	B	C	D	E

(7) $222 \times 333 = 73{,}926$

$73{,}926 \div 111 = F$

What is the value of F?

333	666	445	111	578
A	B	C	D	E

(8) Point D is 3 units north and 4 units west of point C.

What are the coordinates of point D?

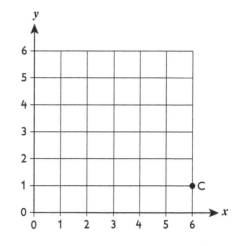

(5, 3)	(3, 6)	(3, 5)	(10, 2)	(2, 4)
A	B	C	D	E

(9) One quarter of a number equals one fifth of 200.

What is the number?

150	180	170	200	160
A	B	C	D	E

Score: .... / 9

51

Test 33

You have 5 minutes to complete this test.

You have 10 questions to complete within the given time.

Draw a line in the box below the correct answer.

EXAMPLE

Round 764 to the nearest 10.

760	750	770	790
⬯	⬯	⬯	⬯

(1) 22,000 visitors, rounded to the nearest 1,000, attended an exhibition.

What is the smallest possible number of visitors who attended the exhibition?

21,500	22,499	21,750	21,000
⬯	⬯	⬯	⬯

(2) What number is missing from the sequence below?

17, 21, ?, 30, 35, 39, 44

25	26	27	28
⬯	⬯	⬯	⬯

(3) A fair die is rolled. What is the probability that it lands on an even number?

$\frac{4}{6}$	$\frac{1}{2}$	$\frac{1}{6}$	$\frac{5}{6}$
⬯	⬯	⬯	⬯

(4) The thermometer on the right shows the daytime temperature in Iceland in degrees.

The temperature drops by 13°C at night.

What is the temperature in Iceland at night?

−26°C	3°C	−23°C	−13°C
⬯	⬯	⬯	⬯

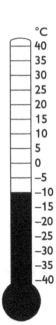

(5) Calculate $\frac{3}{6} + \frac{2}{5}$

$\frac{19}{30}$ ⬭

$\frac{1}{2}$ ⬭

$\frac{22}{30}$ ⬭

$\frac{27}{30}$ ⬭

(6) Adult cinema tickets cost £12 and child tickets cost £6.

An equal number of adult and child tickets are bought.

Which of the following could be the amount that is spent?

£12 ⬭

£20 ⬭

£40 ⬭

£54 ⬭

(7) $2X = \frac{Y}{4}$

If $Y = 8$, what is the value of X?

1 ⬭

2 ⬭

4 ⬭

6 ⬭

(8) Laura spends $3\frac{1}{2}$ hours per day working and 7 hours studying.

What is the ratio of the time Laura spends studying to the time Laura spends working?

3·5:7 ⬭

2:1 ⬭

4:1 ⬭

1:2 ⬭

(9) How many edges does this shape have?

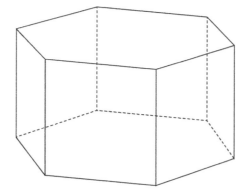

6 ⬭

21 ⬭

18 ⬭

16 ⬭

(10) I spend $2\frac{1}{6}$ hours at the gym.

I leave the gym at 14:22.

At what time did I arrive at the gym?

16:32 ⬭

12:00 ⬭

12:16 ⬭

12:12 ⬭

Score: .... / 10

53

Test 34

Use the shapes below to help you answer the questions in this test. Write the correct answer in the boxes provided (one digit per box).

Shape 1   Shape 2   Shape 3

Not drawn to scale

Shapes 1, 2 and 3 are all regular polygons.

(1) Shape 2 has a perimeter of 43·74 cm.

What is the side length of Shape 2?

☐ · ☐ ☐ cm

(2) What is the sum of the internal angles in Shape 1?

☐ ☐ ☐ °

(3) What is the measure of an exterior angle in Shape 2?

☐ ☐ °

(4) What is the product of the number of sides of Shapes 1, 2 and 3?

☐ ☐ ☐

(5) 6 identical equilateral triangles can fit exactly within Shape 2.

What is the perimeter of 1 of these triangles?

☐ ☐ · ☐ ☐ cm

Test 35

You have 4 minutes to complete this test.

You have 7 questions to complete within the given time.

Write the correct answer in the boxes provided (one digit per box).

EXAMPLE

How much greater is 34 grams than 21 grams? | 1 | 3 | g

1. What is the mode of the following set of numbers?

   2·2, 3·1, 4·5, 8·3, 2·2, 4·5, 8·3, 7·1, 2·2

   ☐ · ☐

2. Kira faces northwest and turns clockwise to face southwest.

   Through how many degrees does Kira turn?

   ☐☐☐°

3. Subtract the smallest prime number from the smallest two-digit square number.

   ☐☐

4. The cost of sending a parcel up to 1 kg in weight is £2·50.

   The cost of sending a parcel over 1 kg in weight is £3·50.

   What is the total cost of sending 3 parcels each weighing 750 g and 2 parcels each weighing 999 g?

   £ ☐☐ · ☐☐

5. 3% of all people who visit an online store make a purchase.

   If 600 people visit the online store, how many make a purchase?

   ☐☐

6. Calculate 10 × 0·1 × 100 × 8·4

   ☐☐☐

7. I have 7 green ties, 4 blue ties and 5 red ties.

   If I pick 1 tie at random, what is the probability that I do not pick a red tie?

   ☐☐
   ――
   ☐☐

Score: .... / 7

Test 36

You have **5 minutes** to complete this test.

You have **10 questions** to complete within the given time.

Circle the letter below the correct answer.

Round 676 to the nearest 10.

680	670	675	690
Ⓐ	B	C	D

---

1 What is the name of this quadrilateral?

parallelogram	trapezium	kite	rhombus
A	B	C	D

2 How many eighths are there in $12\frac{1}{4}$?

96	64	98	50
A	B	C	D

3 3 children took a test. There were 60 marks available.

Tess scored 75%, Bill scored 40% and Gemma scored 90%.

What was the range of their marks?

24	45	54	30
A	B	C	D

4 Michael receives a cash prize of £10,000. Half of it is delivered in £20 notes and the other half is delivered in £50 notes.

How many notes does Michael receive?

10,000	350	500	200
A	B	C	D

5 What is the lowest common multiple of 12 and 8?

48	96	32	24
A	B	C	D

6 A lorry tyre has a circumference of 150 cm.

If the lorry travels 15 km, how many times does the tyre rotate through 360°?

15,000	10,000	1,000	100,000
A	B	C	D

7 In September, the ratio of rainy days to dry days is 2:3.

How many more dry days are there in September than rainy days?

1	12	6	18
A	B	C	D

8 Which number is missing from this sequence?

−0·4, −0·1, ?, 0·5, 0·8

0	2·1	0·2	−0·3
A	B	C	D

9 Figure 1 is an equilateral triangle with a circle inscribed in it.

What is the order of rotational symmetry of Figure 1?

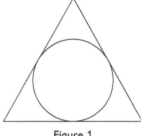

Figure 1

0	1	3	30
A	B	C	D

10 Mia faces northeast. She turns through 3 right angles in a clockwise direction. In which direction does Mia now face?

north	southwest	southeast	northwest
A	B	C	D

Score: .... / 10

Test 37

Draw a line in the box below the correct answer.

EXAMPLE

Round 764 to the nearest 10.

760   750   770   790

---

(1) What is the remainder when 124,896 is divided by 9?

6   4   5   3

(2) What fraction of this shape is not shaded?

$\frac{4}{9}$ $\frac{7}{9}$ $\frac{2}{3}$ $\frac{2}{9}$

(3) Jacob faces northeast and turns 180° anticlockwise.

In which direction does Jacob now face?

northwest   south   east   southwest

(4) What is the difference in value between the largest and smallest of these three expressions?

8 × 9   12 × 5   10 × 11

170   110   50   12

(5) The coordinates of 3 vertices of a square are (2, 6), (2, 2) and (6, 6).

What are the coordinates of the square's 4th vertex?

(6, −2)   (6, 2)   (−2, 2)   (−6, 6)

6 Rob travels 65 km in his van. His van requires 1 litre of petrol to travel 10 km.

Petrol costs £1 per litre.

What is the petrol cost of Rob's 65 km journey?

| £65 | £0·65 | £6 | £6·50 |

7 A watering can contains 2·5 litres of water. Jane uses the can to water her 3 flower beds.

Each flower bed requires $\frac{1}{4}$ litre of water.

How much water remains in the watering can once Jane has finished?

| 1,500 ml | 1,750 ml | 2,000 ml | 2,250 ml |

8 The table below shows the weight of 5 cookies.

What is the range of the weights?

	Weight (g)
Cookie 1	45
Cookie 2	34
Cookie 3	76
Cookie 4	23
Cookie 5	45

| 51 g | 53 g | 47 g | 48 g |

9 A theatre has 3 tiers of seating. Each tier can hold 300 people.

500 people attend a show at the theatre.

What fraction of the theatre is full?

| $\frac{1}{2}$ | $\frac{5}{9}$ | $\frac{3}{5}$ | $\frac{2}{3}$ |

10 A baby elephant drinks $2\frac{1}{4}$ litres of water.

The baby's mother drinks 10 times as much water.

How much water do they drink in total?

| 20·25 litres | 22·5 litres | 21 litres | 24·75 litres |

Score: .... / 10

Test 38

You have 3 minutes to complete this test.

You have 5 questions to complete within the given time.

Use the diagrams below to help you answer the questions in this test. Write the correct answer in the boxes provided (one digit per box).

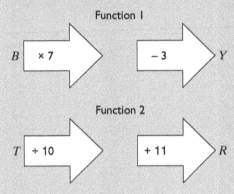

Function 1

B | × 7 → | – 3 → Y

Function 2

T | ÷ 10 → | + 11 → R

The diagrams above show 2 functions.

(1) What is the value of Y when B = 17?

(2) What is the value of T when R = 31?

(3) If Y = 4 and R = 11·1, what is the mean of B and T?

(4) What is the largest possible two-digit value of Y when B is a whole number?

(5) How much greater than R is Y when B = 5 and T = 10?

Score: .... / 5

Test 39

Write the correct answer in the boxes provided (one digit/sign per box).

EXAMPLE

Calculate 17 − 21

$\boxed{-}\ \boxed{4}$

---

1 7 + b + 6 = 5

What is the value of b?

$\boxed{}\ \boxed{}$

2 John receives £4·50 per week of pocket money and Lewis receives £3 per week of pocket money.

How much do they receive in total in 3 weeks?

£ $\boxed{}\ \boxed{}\cdot\boxed{}\ \boxed{}$

3 A plane takes off at 14:48 and lands 2 hours and 27 minutes later.

At what time does the plane land?

$\boxed{}\ \boxed{}:\boxed{}\ \boxed{}$

4 Calculate 3 ÷ 9

Round your answer to 2 decimal places.

$\boxed{}\cdot\boxed{}\ \boxed{}$

5 What is the sum of the internal angles in a rhombus?

$\boxed{}\ \boxed{}\ \boxed{}^{\circ}$

6 What number is missing from this sequence?

74, 69, ?, 62, 60, 59

$\boxed{}\ \boxed{}$

7 A ten-pence coin weighs 7 g.

What is the value of a pile of ten-pence coins that weigh 350 g? £ $\boxed{}\cdot\boxed{}\ \boxed{}$

8 What fraction of month names end with the letter 'y'?

Write your answer as a fraction in its lowest terms.

$\dfrac{\boxed{}}{\boxed{}}$

Score: .... / 8

61

Test 40

You have 5 minutes to complete this test.

You have 10 questions to complete within the given time.

Circle the letter below the correct answer.

EXAMPLE

Round 676 to the nearest 10.

680	670	675	690	650
Ⓐ	B	C	D	E

---

(1) Point B marks the centre of Circle A.

What is the diameter of Circle A?

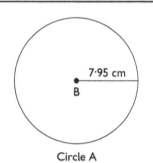

7·95 cm

B

Not drawn to scale

Circle A

14·95 cm	15·9 cm	14·2 cm	7·95 cm	11·7 cm
A	B	C	D	E

(2) What is the sum of the number of dots on a fair die?

6	11	21	8	20
A	B	C	D	E

(3) 7 ☐ 4 + 25 = 769

What digit should be placed in the box to complete the sum correctly?

2	4	6	9	7
A	B	C	D	E

(4) Each month, the price of a dress increased by 10% from the previous month.

If the dress cost £20 in January, how much did it cost in March?

£22	£24	£23·40	£21·11	£24·20
A	B	C	D	E

(5) Chloe must pay 20% of her income in tax.

If Chloe receives an after-tax income of £480, how much tax did she pay?

£480	£600	£200	£90	£120
A	B	C	D	E

(6) 5 children had to estimate the number of blades of grass in the garden.

Beth estimated 127,700. Sam estimated 126,400. Emma estimated 126,999. Tom estimated 127,456. Sarah estimated 126,750.

There were 127,220 blades of grass in the garden.

Which child had the closest estimate?

Beth	Sam	Emma	Tom	Sarah
A	B	C	D	E

(7) 1 tube of toothpaste used by 4 people lasts for 1 month.

How many tubes are needed for 8 people for 2 months?

2	8	4	16	12
A	B	C	D	E

(8) A can of liquid holds 330 ml. 1 ml weighs 1 g.

What is the weight of the liquid in 6 cans?

1,988 g	1·98 l	1,989 ml	1·98 kg	19·8 kg
A	B	C	D	E

(9) Figure 1 is made from 15 different shapes.

What fraction of these shapes are quadrilaterals?

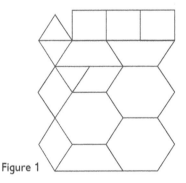

Figure 1

$\frac{2}{15}$	$\frac{11}{15}$	$\frac{8}{15}$	$\frac{3}{5}$	$\frac{1}{15}$
A	B	C	D	E

(10) What is the product of the smallest factor of 7 and the largest factor of 12,000?

84,000	70	7	12,000	21,000
A	B	C	D	E

Score: .... / 10

Test 41

You have 5 minutes to complete this test.

You have 10 questions to complete within the given time.

Draw a line in the box below the correct answer.

EXAMPLE

Round 764 to the nearest 10.

| 760 | 750 | 770 | 790 |

---

1. What type of shape is Figure 1?

Figure 1

| septagon | hexagon | pentagon | quadrilateral |

2. Shape A is made from 2 squares, each with a perimeter of 36 cm.

   What is the perimeter of Shape A?

Not drawn to scale

Shape A

| 36 cm | 63 cm | 72 cm | 54 cm |

3. A tiger runs at a speed of 15 km per hour.

   How far does the tiger run in 4 minutes?

| 5 km | 15 km | 4 km | 1 km |

4 A hotel charges £200 for the first week and then £A per night thereafter.

Which expression shows the cost of staying at the hotel for a fortnight?

200 + 14A 200 − A 200 + 7A 14A − 200

◯   ◯   ◯   ◯

5 How many sevenths are there in $6\frac{2}{7}$?

44   2   42   47

◯   ◯   ◯   ◯

6 There are three times as many boys as girls in the assembly hall.

If there are 96 children in the assembly hall, how many of them are boys?

96   24   72   48

◯   ◯   ◯   ◯

7 What is two hundred thousand and twenty-one less than two hundred thousand, three hundred and seventeen?

312   200,210   296   200,316

◯   ◯   ◯   ◯

8 G and T are two different whole numbers.

$G + T = 17$

$G \times T = 72$

$G < T$

What is the value of G?

11   9   6   8

◯   ◯   ◯   ◯

9 Simon has 5 p.

How many different combinations of coins could Simon have?

4   5   3   1

◯   ◯   ◯   ◯

10 Multiply the largest two-digit prime number by the smallest one-digit prime number.

99   291   194   97

◯   ◯   ◯   ◯

Score: .... / 10

Test 42

You have 3 minutes to complete this test.

You have 5 questions to complete within the given time.

Use the shapes below to help you answer the questions in this test. Write the correct answer in the boxes provided (one digit per box).

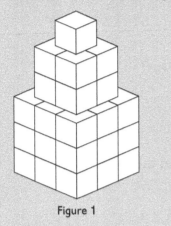

Figure 1

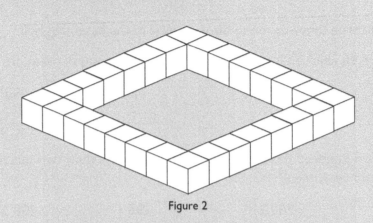

Figure 2

Figures 1 and 2 are formed from identical small cubes, each weighing 2·5 g.

(1) How many small cubes are used to form Figure 2?

(2) Figure 1 is formed from 36 small cubes.

What is twice the weight of Figure 1?

g

(3) The surface of Figure 2 is painted red.

What fraction of all the faces of the small cubes in Figure 2 are now red?

Write your answer as a fraction in its lowest terms.

(4) What is half the weight of Figure 2?

g

(5) Figure 1 consists of a 1 × 1 cube on top of a 2 × 2 cube on top of a 3 × 3 cube.

How many edges does Figure 1 have?

Score: .... / 5

66

Test 43

You have 4 minutes to complete this test.

You have 8 questions to complete within the given time.

Write the correct answer in the boxes provided (one digit per box).

EXAMPLE

How much greater is 34 grams than 21 grams?   [1] [3] g

---

(1) Calculate 0·568 kg + 0·3 kg + 0·04 kg   ☐☐☐ g

(2) 7 builders each work at the same speed. It takes them 4 hours to build a wall.

How long will it take 14 builders to build the same wall, assuming they work at the same speed?   ☐ hours

(3) The ratio of black dogs to white dogs in a park is 3:4.

If 1 dog is picked at random, what is the probability that it is white?   ☐/☐

(4) How many edges does a triangular prism have?   ☐

(5) $7R + 6Y = 4T$

If $R = 4$ and $T = 16$, what is the value of Y?   ☐

(6) Nina has 2 cubes. She paints 2 faces of the first cube red and 3 faces of the second cube red.

What fraction of the 2 cubes' faces are painted red?   ☐/☐☐

(7) Subtract 644 from 1,843.   ☐,☐☐☐

(8) The cost of a phone call is 70 p for the first minute and then 8 p for every minute thereafter.

If a call cost £1·34, for how many minutes did it last?   ☐ mins

Score: .... / 8

67

Test 44

You have **5 minutes** to complete this test.

You have **10 questions** to complete within the given time.

Circle the letter below the correct answer.

EXAMPLE

Round 676 to the nearest 10.

680	670	675	690
Ⓐ	B	C	D

(1) Which of these values is the second largest?

0·545	0·454	0·555	0·455
A	B	C	D

(2) What is twenty-two thousand four hundred and twenty-two more than one thousand eight hundred and ninety-one?

1,891	23,313	22,422	24,313
A	B	C	D

(3) The 3 angles in a triangle are $3X°$, $2X°$ and $4X°$.

What is the value of $X°$?

80°	90°	60°	20°
A	B	C	D

(4) The thermometer on the right shows the temperature in London in degrees.

The temperature in Finland is 22°C colder than the temperature in London.

What is the temperature in Finland?

−13°C	−9°C	7°C	9°C
A	B	C	D

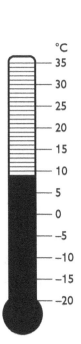

(5) Lily thinks of a number at random between 1 and 100 exclusive.

What is the probability that Lily thinks of a square number?

$\frac{1}{10}$	$\frac{1}{12}$	$\frac{4}{49}$	$\frac{9}{98}$
A	B	C	D

(6) A cheetah runs 22 times faster than a hyena.

How far can a hyena run in the same time that it takes a cheetah to run 444 m?

Select the answer to the nearest metre.

9,768 m	44 m	20 m	21 m
A	B	C	D

(7) Calculate 745,000 × 0·0001

7,450,000	7,450	74,500	74·5
A	B	C	D

(8) Multiply the number of circles in this diagram by 7.

12	84	56	98
A	B	C	D

(9) Fred bakes muffins and places them on plates to be served. He places 6 muffins on each plate and he has 5 muffins left over.

How many muffins could Fred have baked?

42	53	76	91
A	B	C	D

(10) A light bulb lasts 27 days.

How many light bulbs were needed to last 9 months from January to September 2013?

8	9	10	11
A	B	C	D

Score: .... / 10

Test 45

You have 3 minutes to complete this test.

You have 5 questions to complete within the given time.

Use the images below to help you answer the questions in this test. Write the correct answer in the boxes provided (one digit per box).

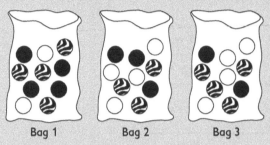

Bag 1   Bag 2   Bag 3

Each bag contains black, white and striped marbles.

1 If a marble is selected at random from **Bag 2**, what is the probability that it is black?

Write your answer as a fraction in its lowest terms.

2 If a black marble is removed from **Bag 3** and then a marble is selected at random from **Bag 3**, what is the probability that it is white?

Write your answer as a fraction in its lowest terms.

3 If the contents of **Bags 1** and **3** are mixed and then a marble is selected at random, what is the probability that it is striped?

Write your answer as a fraction in its lowest terms.

4 If the contents of all 3 bags are mixed and then a marble is selected at random, what is the probability that it is white?

Write your answer as a fraction in its lowest terms.

5 If all the black marbles are removed from **Bag 1** and then a marble is selected at random from **Bag 2**, what is the probability that it is striped?

Write your answer as a fraction in its lowest terms.

Score: .... / 5

Answers

Key abbreviations: °C: degrees centigrade, b: base, cm: centimetre, d.p.: decimal place, g: gram, h: height, kg: kilogram, km: kilometre, kph: kilometres per hour, l: litre, LCM: lowest common multiple, m: metre, mins: minutes, ml: millilitre, mm: millimetre, R: remainder

Test 1

Q1 4,146
3,423 + 723 = 4,146

Q2 719
6,471 ÷ 9 = 719

Q3 3,217,001

Q4 6,675
The rule of the sequence is +25, so the next number is: 6,650 + 25 = 6,675

Q5 −2°C
12°C + 5°C = 17°C; 17°C − 19°C = −2°C

Q6 £9·32
34 p × 2 = 68 p; £10 − £0·68 = £9·32

Q7 2
Shape holds same form twice when rotated 360°

Q8 81
$X = 27 × 3 = 81$

Q9 40
Sum of prime numbers = 23 + 17 = 40

Q10 $3\frac{2}{3}$
$\frac{33}{9} = 3\frac{2}{3}$

Test 2

Q1 74
74 in the pasta circle but not in the pizza circle

Q2 41
41 in neither circle

Q3 15
150 − 74 − 20 − 41 = 15

Q4 $\frac{2}{15}$
$\frac{20}{150} = \frac{2}{15}$

Q5 25
35 children like pizza, so $\frac{2}{7}$ of 35 = 10; 35 − 10 = 25

Test 3

Q1 (0, 0)
The square has a side length of 4 units

Q2 147
21 × 7 = 147

Q3 16
31 days in January
Bill waters his plants on all odd days so 16 times

Q4 54·68
7 in the tenths column rounds up to 8 as the digit in the hundredths column is 8

Q5 15
56 − 56 + 15 = 15

Q6 1,200
1·2 m = 120 cm = 1,200 mm

Q7 91
Cost of 1 plate = £39 ÷ 3 = £13; £13 × 7 = £91

Q8 28
54 + 30 = 84; 84 ÷ 3 = 28

Q9 34
Robert is 136 cm tall
Henry is 102 cm tall
Sam is 116 cm tall
136 cm − 102 cm = 34 cm

Test 4

Q1 B
Twice the area = 2((b × h) ÷ 2) = b × h = 7 cm × 8 cm = 56 cm²

Q2 A
10 × 7 = 70

Q3 B
16, 25, 36, 49, 64, 81

Q4 A
$\frac{1}{3}$ of £120 = £40; £120 − £40 − £20 = £60
£60 is 50% of £120

Q5 A
225 = 45% so 5 = 1% so 500 = 100%

Q6 D
If there were 99 players, then 77 would be right-footed, so 76 is the best estimate.

Q7 C
A to B = $3X$; B to C = X; $4X$ = 24 cm so X = 6 cm

Q8 D
1 side of hexagon = 42 ÷ 6 = 7 cm
Figure 1 has 16 sides so perimeter = 16 cm × 7 = 112 cm

Test 5

Q1 3
Factors: 1, 3, 9

Q2 36
108 ÷ 3 = 36

Q3 64
24 is eight times greater than 3 so 8 × 8 = 64

Q4 16 cm
Length = √16 = 4 cm; perimeter = 4 × 4 = 16 cm

Test 5 answers continue on next page

Q5   **2:1:1**

If Anna receives $2X$, Kate and Sarah both receive X
so Anna:Sarah:Kate = $2X$:$1X$:$1X$ = 2:1:1

Q6   **0·84**

7 × 12 cm = 84 cm = 0·84 m

Q7 $\frac{1}{6}$

6 equally possible outcomes so $\frac{1}{6}$

Q8   **189 g**

9 × 3 g = 27 g per day; 27 g × 7 = 189 g per week

Q9   **10:41**

Time in Delhi is 17:11; $6\frac{1}{2}$ hours before 17:11 is 10:41

Q10   **£18·75**

50% of £12·50 = £6·25; £12·50 + £6·25 = £18·75

Test 6

Q1   **19·5**

AB is twice the length of 1 side of a triangle so
13 cm ÷ 2 = 6·5 cm
6·5 cm × 3 = 19·5 cm

Q2   **3**

Figure 2 repeats its form three times when rotated
through 360°

Q3   **21**

Figure 2 is an equilateral triangle so 7 cm × 3 = 21 cm

Q4   **42·9**

Perimeter of hexagon = 6·5 cm × 6 = 39 cm
10% of 39 cm = 3·9 cm; 39 cm + 3·9 cm = 42·9 cm

Q5   **11**

Perimeter of Figure 2 = 21 cm
21 cm ÷ 2 = 10·5 seconds
10·5 seconds = 11 seconds (rounded to nearest whole
number)

Test 7

Q1   **360**

3,240 ÷ 9 = 360

Q2   **10**

Dividing by 0·5 is the same as multiplying by 2
$5 \div \frac{1}{2} = 5 \times 2 = 10$

Q3   **37**

Each term after the first and second terms is the
sum of the 2 previous terms:
23 + 14 = 37

Q4   **60**

20% of 200 = 40 yellow lizards
$\frac{1}{4}$ of 160 = 40 black lizards
200 − 40 − 40 = 120
$\frac{120}{200} \times 100$ = 60%

Q5   **16**

Half of 34 = 17; $\frac{1}{3}$ of 45 = 15
The whole number is in between 15 and 17, so it is 16

Q6   **408**

£34 × 12 = £408

Q7   **0**

Total score = average × number of scores = 6 × 4 = 24
G = 24 − 12 − 3 − 9 = 0

Q8   **3·60**

12 × £1·50 = £18; 20% of £18 = £3·60

Test 8

Q1   **B**

$\frac{19}{6} = 3\frac{1}{6}$; $\frac{14}{5} = 2\frac{4}{5}$; $\frac{21}{7} = 3$; $\frac{30}{9} = 3\frac{1}{9}$; $\frac{40}{4} = 10$
So $\frac{14}{5} < 3$

Q2   **C**

21 minutes before 9:30 a.m. is 9:09 a.m.
6:21 a.m. to 9:09 a.m. is 2 h 48 mins

Q3   **A**

LCM of 4 and 5 is 20 so 20th, 40th, 60th, 80th and
100th person

Q4   **E**

78 ÷ 7 = 11 R 1

Q5   **B**

Right angle is a 90° angle

Q6   **D**

Cost of purchase = £5 − £3·70 = £1·30; 3 pens = £0·90
So 2 pencils = £0·40
So 1 pencil = £0·20

Q7   **A**

$2(4^2)$ = 2 × 16 = 32; 32 − 1 = 31

Q8   **D**

If the area of the grey circle is twice the area of the
white circle, then the grey area of Figure 2 is equal to
the white area, so the answer is 50%

Q9   **A**

Number must be 4 greater than a multiple of 7 so 53

Q10   **E**

5th side = 17 cm − 3·5 cm − 2·2 cm − 1·9 cm − 6·7 cm
= 2·7 cm

Test 9

Q1   **4**

Perimeter of G = 11 cm + 11 cm + 6 cm + 6 cm = 34 cm
So 34 cm = 13 cm + 13 cm + $2X$ so $2X$ = 8 cm
So X = 4 cm

Q2   **1·5**

$\frac{9}{6} = 1\frac{3}{6} = 1\frac{1}{2} = 1·5$

Q3   **£1·32**

Cost of 1 apple = 88 ÷ 8 = 11 p
12 × 11 = 132 p = £1·32

Q4   **1**

Q5   **10**

Sum of 3 smallest prime numbers = 2 + 3 + 5 = 10

Q6   **0·6**

60 seconds in 1 minute so 60 × 1 cm per second = 60 cm
per minute = 0·6 metres per minute

Q7 3,864
322 × 12 = 3,864

Q8 36
1 day = 24 hours; $\frac{1}{2}$ day = 12 hours; 24 + 12 = 36

Q9 $\frac{1}{6}$
$\frac{1}{2} + \frac{1}{3} = \frac{3}{6} + \frac{2}{6} = \frac{5}{6}$; $1 - \frac{5}{6} = \frac{1}{6}$

Q10 93
January = 31 days; 31 × 3 = 93

Test 10

Q1 3 53
14:07 to 18:00 is 3 hours and 53 minutes

Q2 15:21
74 minutes after 14:07 is 15:21

Q3 21:12
$3\frac{1}{5}$ hours is 3 hours 12 minutes
So Jill goes to bed at 21:12

Q4 10 22
21:12 to 07:34 is 10 hours and 22 minutes

Q5 180
Hands form a straight line, so the angle formed is 180°

Test 11

Q1 34
34 is the only number that appears twice

Q2 30
Perimeter = 8 × 7·5 cm = 60 cm; half of 60 cm = 30 cm

Q3 26
$(1 + 3)^2 + 1^2 + 3^2 = 16 + 1 + 9 = 26$

Q4 29
£1·45 = 145 p; 145 ÷ 5 = 29

Q5 1·4
3·5 × 400 m = 1,400 m; 1,400 m = 1·4 km

Q6 $\frac{1}{9}$
9 pieces of paper; so $\frac{1}{9}$

Q7 2·8
$\frac{14}{5} = 2\frac{4}{5} = 2\cdot8$

Q8 45·6
100 × 4·56 = 456; 456 × 0·1 = 45·6

Q9 75
Percentage increase = (increase ÷ original price) × 100
So (6 ÷ 8) × 100 = 75%

Q10 240
1 angle in an equilateral triangle is 60°
60° × 2 = 120°; 2 × 120° = 240°

Test 12

Q1 D
Factors of 100: 1, 100, 2, 50, 4, 25, 5, 20, 10

Q2 B
Each division represents 250 ml hence container holds
1,500 ml = 1·5 l

Q3 C
180° − 74° − 81° = 25°

Q4 D
2 m 24 cm = 224 cm; 224 ÷ 4 = 56 cm; 56 × 3 = 168 cm

Q5 C
Divide both sides by 5; 13:9

Q6 C
The shape holds the same form twice when rotated
through 360°

Q7 B
Each term is 0·04 less than the previous term
0·97 − 0·04 = 0·93

Q8 D
24 hours in a day; $\frac{7}{12} = \frac{14}{24}$ so lights turned on for
14 hours

Q9 A
10% of £11·10 = £1·11; £11·10 − £1·11 = £9·99

Q10 C
2·56 kg × 1,000 = 2,560 g so 2,564 g is the largest
possible number

Test 13

Q1 1,092
6,101 − 5,009 = 1,092

Q2 8
817 + 358 = 1,175

Q3 11
Test the options: $A = 11$; $B = 4$

Q4 86 cm
8 × 6 cm = 48 cm
1 m 34 cm − 48 cm = 134 cm − 48 cm = 86 cm

Q5 $\frac{1}{7}$
2 weeks = 14 days; $\frac{2}{14} = \frac{1}{7}$

Q6 18:44
3 hours 21 minutes after 15:23 is 18:44

Q7 34
Sequence is adding increasing square numbers: +1, +4,
+9, +16, +25

Q8 44
4 cm cube will be made from 4 × 4 × 4 = 64 blocks
64 − 20 = 44

Q9 $\frac{4}{20}$
$\frac{4}{10} = 0\cdot4$; $\frac{4}{20} = \frac{2}{10} = 0\cdot2$
0·2 < 0·4 < 0·423 < 0·45
So $\frac{4}{20}$ is the smallest

Q10 97%
Total score = 95% × 3 = 285%
Third test score = 285% − 94% − 94% = 97%

Test 14

Q1 **Fred**
Oldest to youngest: Ted, Fred, Adam, Simon

Q2 **32**
11th July to 12th August is 32 days

Q3 **Wednesday**
11th July to 19th July is 8 days, so 8 days after Tuesday is Wednesday

Q4 **7th**
Counting days only, Adam's sister is 5 days older so 5 days before the 12th is the 7th

Q5 $\frac{1}{3}$
4 out of 12 months have 30 days: April, June, September, November
$\frac{4}{12} = \frac{1}{3}$

Test 15

Q1 **900**
1% = 6,000 ÷ 100 = 60; so 15% = 15 × 60 = 900
or $6{,}000 \times \frac{15}{100} = 900$

Q2 **126**
4th angle = 360° − 234° = 126°

Q3 $\frac{1}{3}$
Cube has 6 faces; $\frac{2}{6} = \frac{1}{3}$

Q4 **36**
17 + 19 = 36

Q5 **1**

Q6 **24**
6 × 18 p = 108 p; 108 p ÷ 9 = 12 p; 12 p × 2 = 24 p

Q7 **8**

Q8 **1·8**
20% of 18 = 3·6; 50% of 3·6 = 1·8

Test 16

Q1 **E**
325 × 25 = 8,125

Q2 **B**
5 a.m. to 6 p.m. = 13 hours; 13 × 3°C = 39°C;
−3°C + 39°C = 36°C

Q3 **D**
$\frac{1}{4}$ of £4·20 = £1·05; £4·20 + £1·05 = £5·25

Q4 **D**
Removing a square with a width of 1 cm from each corner does not change the perimeter of the 5 cm × 5 cm square so perimeter of Figure 1 = 5 cm × 4 = 20 cm

Q5 **B**
Total burgers sold = 22 × 7 = 154
So burgers sold on Tuesday = 154 − 19 − 23 − 21 − 22 − 24 − 18 = 27

Q6 **A**
13 is the only prime number; so $\frac{1}{7}$

Q7 **C**
15 mins is $\frac{1}{4}$ of an hour; $\frac{1}{4}$ of 40 km = 10 km

Q8 **E**
7 out of 10 visitors are adults so in 30 visitors there are 21 adults; 21 × £5 = £105

Q9 **B**
At 12 p.m.: 1 × 3 = 3 cells; at 1 p.m.: 3 × 3 = 9 cells; at 2 p.m.: 9 × 3 = 27 cells

Q10 **B**
The 7 is in the hundreds columns so it represents a value of 700

Test 17

Q1 $\frac{1}{2}$
$\frac{2}{6} = \frac{1}{3}$; $\frac{3}{9} = \frac{1}{3}$; so $\frac{1}{2}$ is the greatest

Q2 **9**
3 rows: 5 on the first row, 3 on the second row, 1 on the third row; 5 + 3 + 1 = 9

Q3 **19**
Day 1 = 9; day 2 = 11; day 3 = 13; day 4 = 15; day 5 = 17; day 6 = 19

Q4 **750**
(105,000,000 ÷ 70,000) ÷ 2 = A; so 1,500 ÷ 2 = A
So A = 750

Q5 **54**
3✤ = (3 × 3) + 45 = 9 + 45 = 54

Q6 **2 cm**
The sum of the lengths of any 2 sides of a triangle must be greater than the length of the third side.

Q7 **55**
$\frac{1}{2} \times \frac{1}{2} \times \frac{1}{2} \times 440 = 55 = S$

Q8 **172**
90 + 18 + 64 = 172

Q9 **45°**
Opposite angles in a parallelogram are equal.

Q10 **40 p**
Let a = apples and o = oranges
$3a + 4o = 2{\cdot}50$
$2a + 4o = 2{\cdot}20$
Subtract one equation from the other so a = 0·30
So 3(0·30) + 4o = 2·50
So 4o = 1·60
So o = 0·40 so cost of 1 orange is 40 p

Test 18

Q1 $\frac{1}{5}$
3 is the only prime number so $\frac{1}{5}$

Q2 **9,943**
4 largest cards arranged in descending order: 9, 9, 4, 3

Q3 **85,932**
Largest number: 99,431; smallest number: 13,499
99,431 − 13,499 = 85,932

Q4 **5·2**
(4 + 3 + 9 + 9 + 1) ÷ 5 = 5·2

Q5 **6**

$(9 + 9) \div (1 \times 3) = 18 \div 3 = 6$

Test 19

Q1 **8**

14:07, 14:14, 14:21, 14:28, 14:35, 14:42, 14:49, 14:56

Q2 **25**

Percentage decrease = 2,000 ÷ 8,000 × 100 = 25%

Q3 **£6·00**

$9 ÷ $1·50 = £6·00

Q4 $\frac{2}{3}$

Uncovered area = 36 cm² − 12 cm² = 24 cm²;

$\frac{24 \text{ cm}^2}{36 \text{ cm}^2} = \frac{2}{3}$

Q5 **2**

1 cm on map represents 100,000 cm

100,000 cm = 1,000 m = 1 km

So 2 cm on map = 2 km

Q6 **0**

There are 4 right angles in a square and no right angles in an equilateral triangle

$4 \times 0 = 0$

Q7 **5**

89 ÷ 22 = 4 R 1; so 5 containers are needed

Q8 **539**

7 × 77 = 539

Test 20

Q1 **B**

Total seats = (74 × 6) − 2 = 442

Q2 **C**

Length = (44 cm − 7 cm − 7 cm) ÷ 2 = 30 cm ÷ 2 = 15 cm

Q3 **C**

Side length of hexagon = 42 cm ÷ 6 = 7 cm

So perimeter of octagon = 7 cm × 8 = 56 cm

Q4 **D**

None of the coins in his pocket has an odd value so the probability is 0

Q5 **D**

$5·6; 5\frac{7}{10} = 5·7; \frac{35}{7} = 5; \frac{18}{3} = 6$

$6 > 5·7 > 5·6 > 5$ so $\frac{18}{3}$ has the largest value

Q6 **B**

$R° = 360° − 95° − 78° − 123° = 64°$

Q7 **D**

3·5 cm = 35 mm

Q8 **C**

5 + 6 + 7 = 18; 5 × 6 × 7 = 210

Q9 **A**

100% − 60% − 35% = 5%; 5% of 1,000 = 50

Q10 **A**

3(3·3 − 2·7) + 4 = 3(0·6) + 4 = 1·8 + 4 = 5·8

Test 21

Q1 **−0·9**

2·345 − 3·245 = −0·9

Q2 **0·468 kg**

7 × 76 g = 532 g = 0·532 kg; 1 kg − 0·532 kg = 0·468 kg

Q3 **6·3 cm**

45 ÷ 5 = 9 coins; 9 × 7 mm = 63 mm = 6·3 cm

Q4 **36 m²**

9 cm × 4 cm represents 900 cm × 400 cm = 9 m × 4 m = 36 m²

Q5 **12 cm**

Area = (b × h) ÷ 2; so 42 = 7b ÷ 2; so 7b = 84; so b = 12 cm

Q6 **30°**

$r° = 360° ÷ 12 = 30°$

Q7 $\frac{2}{3}$

Monkey 1 receives 2 out of 3 parts so $\frac{2}{3}$

Q8 **0**

0 is the only value that satisfies the equation

Q9 **40**

3 years ago, Rahul's father was 35 years old; today he is 38 years old and in 2 years' time he will be 40

Q10 **41**

7 × 8 = 56; 7 + 8 = 15; 56 − 15 = 41

Test 22

Q1 **northwest**

45° is half of a quarter turn so Malik faces northwest

Q2 **270**

Turning from east to north is 3 right angle turns so bearing is 270°

Q3 **7**

5 m east and 5 m west cancel each other out so Mark is 7 m north of his starting point

Q4 **northwest**

From northeast, 3 right angle clockwise turns faces northwest

Q5 $\frac{3}{8}$

$\frac{135°}{360°} = \frac{3}{8}$

Test 23

Q1 **20**

Area of square = 4 cm × 4 cm = 16 cm²

Area of rectangle = 16 cm × 20 cm = 320 cm²

320 cm² ÷ 16 cm² = 20

Q2 **96**

32 × 3 = 96

Q3 **113**

2·24 m − 111 cm = 224 cm − 111 cm = 113 cm

Q4 **£5·95**

45 p × 11 = £4·95; 25 p × 4 = £1; £4·95 + £1 = £5·95

Test 23 answers continue on next page

Q5 1
5th side = 15 cm − 4·5 cm − 2 cm − 5 cm − 2·5 cm = 1 cm

Q6 16:25
90 minutes ÷ 2 = 45 minutes
45 minutes after 15:40 is 16:25

Q7 4
7 − 3 = 4

Q8 7
Prime factors of 35 are 5 and 7

Test 24

Q1 B
4·743 + 47·43 = 52·173

Q2 E
30 = 25% so 120 = 100%; 120 − 30 = 90

Q3 B
Largest factor = 4,000; smallest factor = 1;
4,000 − 1 = 3,999

Q4 C
$\frac{1}{5}$ of an hour = 12 mins; $\frac{1}{6}$ of an hour = 10 mins;
12 − 10 = 2 mins = 120 seconds

Q5 A
1 box costs (£63 ÷ 9) = £7; £7 ÷ 35 = 20 p

Q6 B
3 km per day; 3 km × 7 = 21 km

Q7 A
Area of rectangle = 52·5 cm² − 10·5 cm² = 42 cm²
So X cm = area ÷ width = 42 ÷ 7 = 6 cm

Q8 A
Side length of Square A = 4 cm
Side length of Square B = 1·25 × 4 cm = 5 cm
Perimeter of Square B = 5 cm × 4 = 20 cm

Q9 C
180° − 70° − 55° = 55°, so the angles in the triangle
are 55°, 55° and 70°
2 angles are equal, therefore it is an isosceles triangle

Q10 E
Time shown is 07:10
15 hours 34 mins after 07:10 is 22:44

Test 25

Q1 £11·41
£15 − £1·30 − £1·30 − £0·99 = £11·41

Q2 140 cm²
Area of Rectangle B = 10 cm × 14 cm = 140 cm²

Q3 120
4 + 5 + 6 = 15 so 4 × 5 × 6 = 120

Q4 $\frac{1}{10}$
2 hours = 120 minutes; $\frac{12}{120} = \frac{1}{10}$

Q5 4·09 m
Range = greatest − smallest
411 cm − 20 mm = 411 cm − 2 cm = 409 cm = 4·09 m

Q6 105
Right angle = 90°; $\frac{90}{360} = \frac{1}{4}$; 420 ÷ 4 = 105

Q7 12
3 × 4 = 12

Q8 $\frac{7}{20}$
$\frac{4}{5}$ = 0·8; $\frac{7}{20}$ = 0·35; 0·35 < 0·8 < 0·81 < 0·82
So $\frac{7}{20}$ is the smallest

Q9 9 minutes
Train A: 29 minutes; Train B: 38 minutes
38 − 29 = 9 minutes

Q10 17:43
In 2 hours, the watch gains 4 minutes
2 hours and 4 minutes after 15:39 is 17:43

Test 26

Q1 150
Area = 6 × 25 cm² = 150 cm²

Q2 56
Side length of 1 square = 16 ÷ 4 = 4 cm
There are 14 sides in Figure 1 so 14 × 4 cm = 56 cm

Q3 $\frac{2}{3}$
The ratio is 1:2 so 2 out of 3, or $\frac{2}{3}$, parts are painted
blue

Q4 0

Q5 576
Area = 6(6 × 16 cm²) = 6 × 96 cm² = 576 cm²

Test 27

Q1 16
Total score for 3 tests = 12 × 3 = 36
Total score for 4 tests = 13 × 4 = 52
52 − 36 = 16

Q2 20
1 p + 2 p = 3 p; 30 ÷ 3 = 10 so 10 two-pence coins and
10 one-pence coins so 20 coins in total

Q3 9·10
Cost of one lemon = 770 p ÷ 11 = 70 p
70 p × 13 = 910 p = £9·10

Q4 60
$\frac{15}{25} = \frac{60}{100}$ = 60%

Q5 8
$\frac{17}{34} = \frac{1}{2} = \frac{4}{8}$; so V = 8

Q6 0·075
7·5 ÷ 100 = 0·075

Q7 110
20 × 4 = 80; 5 × 6 = 30; 80 + 30 = 110

Test 28

Q1 **B**
20, 22, 24, 26, 28, 30

Q2 **D**
Triangle is isosceles so angles are 68°, 68° and 44°
$b°$ is the exterior angle so $b° = 180° - 44° = 136°$

Q3 **D**
7·75 m − 3·25 m = 4·5 m; 4·5 m ÷ 0·5 m = 9

Q4 **C**
9 people in total; 9 × 200 g = 1,800 g = 1·8 kg

Q5 **B**
Rick receives 1 part from 5 so $\frac{1}{5}$ = 20%

Q6 **C**
3rd term = 6 + 1 = 7; 5th term = 10 + 1 = 11
7 + 11 = 18

Q7 **A**
$8(2X - 2) = 16X - 16$

Q8 **C**
There are 11 small black circles and 5 large black circles
$(11 × 1·5 \text{ cm}^2) + (5 × 2·5 \text{ cm}^2) = 16·5 \text{ cm}^2 + 12·5 \text{ cm}^2$
$= 29 \text{ cm}^2$

Q9 **D**
9 × 250 ml = 2·25 litres per hour; 2·25 × 3 = 6·75 litres;
7 − 6·75 = 0·25 litres

Q10 **A**
Largest number = 333; smallest number = 223
Difference = 333 − 223 = 110

Test 29

Q1 **7**
84 ÷ 12 = 7

Q2 **718**
674 + 43 + 234 − 233 = 718

Q3 **2 p**
5 × 5 p = 25 p; 27 p − 25 p = 2 p

Q4 **52·7688**
0·756 × 69·8 = 52·7688

Q5 **120**
$\frac{1}{4}$ of 240 = 60; 240 − 60 = 180; $\frac{1}{3}$ of 180 = 60;
180 − 60 = 120

Q6 **39 kph**
20 minutes × 3 = 1 hour; 13 km × 3 = 39 km
So car's speed is 39 kph

Q7 **5**

Q8 **56 cm**
Side length of each square = 16 cm ÷ 4 = 4 cm
Shape A has 14 sides; 14 × 4 cm = 56 cm

Q9 **0·00001**
1 km = 1,000 m = 100,000 cm
So 1 ÷ 100,000 = 0·00001

Q10 **£136**
9 a.m. to 5·30 p.m. = 8·5 hours
8·5 × 2 = 17; 17 × £8 = £136

Test 30

Q1 **(−1, 5)**
Reflection in y-axis so x coordinate becomes negative

Q2 **(1, −5)**
Reflection in x-axis so y coordinate becomes negative

Q3 **5**
Area = (b × h) ÷ 2 = (2 × 5) ÷ 2 = 10 ÷ 2 = 5 cm^2

Q4 **6**
Diagonally opposite vertices of (−2, 1) and (−4, 4)
create a rectangle with sides of 2 cm and 3 cm
So area = (b × h) = 2 × 3 = 6 cm^2

Q5 **(−3, 0)**
5 units down and 4 units to the left

Test 31

Q1 **48**
4 × 12 = 48

Q2 **28**
This year, George is 9 so Vic is: 9 × 3 = 27 years old
Next year, Vic will be 28 years old.

Q3 **0·08**
$\frac{2}{5}$ of 25 p = 10 p; so 25 p − 10 p − 7 p = 8 p = £0·08

Q4 **230**
300 − 70 = 230

Q5 **8**

Q6 **90**
$4x = 60$ so $x = 15$; 4th term is $6x$; 6 × 15 = 90

Q7 **(4, 4)**
Halfway between the points is (4, 4)

Q8 **7**
6 × 75 ml = 450 ml; 7 × 75 ml = 525 ml
So 7 bottles needed

Test 32

Q1 **D**
$17 + 2 − 8 + 21 = 32$; $G × 2 = 32$; so $G = 16$

Q2 **C**
£9 × 3 = £27 per day; 27th June to 10th July is 14 days
14 × £27 = £378

Q3 **A**
There are 6 ahead of her and 17 behind her; 17 + 6 = 23

Q4 **E**
Test each possibility: 102 ÷ 2 = 51; 51 − 17 = 34;
51 + 17 = 68; 68 is twice 34

Q5 **C**
75,643 ÷ 7 = 10,806 R 1

Q6 **D**

Test 32 answers continue on next page

Q7 **B**
111 is half of 222; so F will be twice 333, which is 666

Q8 **E**

Q9 **E**
Let the number = X
$\frac{1}{5}$ of 200 = 40 so $\frac{1}{4}$ of X = 40 so X = 40 × 4 =160

Test 33

Q1 **21,500**
21,500 is the smallest number that rounds up to 22,000

Q2 **26**
The rule of the sequence is +4, +5, +4, +5 …

Q3 $\frac{1}{2}$
There are 6 possibilities, 3 of which are even: 2, 4, 6
So $\frac{3}{6} = \frac{1}{2}$

Q4 **−23°C**
−10°C − 13°C = −23°C

Q5 $\frac{27}{30}$
$\frac{3}{6} + \frac{2}{5} = \frac{15}{30} + \frac{12}{30} = \frac{27}{30}$

Q6 **£54**
1 adult ticket + 1 child ticket = £12 + £6 = £18
Total amount spent needs to be a multiple of £18, so the answer is £54

Q7 **1**
$2X = 2$ so $X = 1$

Q8 **2:1**
7:3·5 = 2:1

Q9 **18**

Q10 **12:12**
$2\frac{1}{6}$ hours = 2 hours 10 minutes; so 12:12

Test 34

Q1 **7·29**
43·74 cm ÷ 6 = 7·29 cm

Q2 **540**
Sum of internal angles = 180° × (number of sides − 2) = 180° × 3 = 540°

Q3 **60**
Internal angle = 720° ÷ 6 = 120°
Exterior angle = 180° − interior angle = 180° − 120° = 60°

Q4 **240**
5 × 6 × 8 = 240

Q5 **21·87**
Side length of equilateral triangle = side length of Shape 2 = 7·29 cm
So perimeter of equilateral triangle = 7·29 cm × 3 = 21·87 cm

Test 35

Q1 **2·2**
2·2 occurs three times

Q2 **270**
Turn through 3 right angles so 3 × 90° = 270°

Q3 **14**
16 − 2 = 14

Q4 **£12·50**
5 parcels all under 1 kg; so 5 × £2·50 = £12·50

Q5 **18**
1% of 600 = 6; so 3% = 18

Q6 **840**
10 × 0·1 × 100 × 8·4 = 100 × 8·4 = 840

Q7 $\frac{11}{16}$
16 ties in total; 11 are not red so $\frac{11}{16}$

Test 36

Q1 **B**

Q2 **C**
$12\frac{1}{4} = 12\frac{2}{8} = \frac{98}{8}$

Q3 **D**
Tess scored 45 marks; Bill scored 24 marks; Gemma scored 54 marks; 54 − 24 = 30

Q4 **B**
£5,000 ÷ £20 = 250; £5,000 ÷ £50 = 100;
100 + 250 = 350

Q5 **D**
Factors of 12 = 2 × 2 × 3; factors of 8 = 2 × 2 × 2 so LCM = 2 × 2 × 2 × 3 = 24

Q6 **B**
15 km = 15,000 m = 1,500,000 cm
1,500,000 cm ÷ 150 cm = 10,000

Q7 **C**
30 days in September; number of rainy days = $\frac{2}{5}$ = 12; number of dry days = $\frac{3}{5}$ = 18; 18 − 12 = 6

Q8 **C**
Each term is 0·3 greater than the previous term, so:
−0·1 + 0·3 = 0·2

Q9 **C**
Figure 1 repeats itself three times when rotated through 360°

Q10 **D**
3 right angles represents a 270° turn clockwise so northwest

Test 37

Q1 **3**
124,896 ÷ 9 = 13,877 R 3

Q2 $\frac{7}{9}$
2 out of 9 parts are shaded so $\frac{7}{9}$ parts are not shaded

Q3 **southwest**
180° is a half turn; half turn from northeast is southwest

Q4 **50**
8 × 9 = 72; 12 × 5 = 60; 10 × 11 = 110
110 − 60 = 50

Q5 **(6, 2)**
Length of each side is 4 units so (6, 2)

Q6 **£6·50**

65 ÷ 10 = 6·5 required; 6·5 × £1 = £6·50

Q7 **1,750 ml**

$\frac{1}{4}$ litre = 250 ml; 3 × 250 ml = 750 ml

2,500 ml − 750 ml = 1,750 ml

Q8 **53 g**

Range = greatest − smallest = 76 g − 23 g = 53 g

Q9 $\frac{5}{9}$

Theatre capacity = 300 × 3 = 900; $\frac{500}{900} = \frac{5}{9}$

Q10 **24·75 litres**

$2\frac{1}{4}$ litres = 2·25 litres; 2·25 litres × 10 = 22·5 litres;

22·5 litres + 2·25 litres = 24·75 litres

Test 38

Q1 **116**

17 × 7 = 119; 119 − 3 = 116

Q2 **200**

Work backwards: 31 − 11 = 20; 20 × 10 = 200

Q3 **1**

$B = (4 + 3) ÷ 7 = 1$; $T = (11·1 − 11) × 10 = 1$

The mean of 1 and 1 is 1

Q4 **95**

If $B = 14$, $Y = 95$; if $B = 15$, $Y = 102$

So 95 is the largest possible two-digit value of Y

Q5 **20**

If $B = 5$, $Y = 32$; if $T = 10$, $R = 12$

32 − 12 = 20

Test 39

Q1 **−8**

$b = 5 − 7 − 6 = −8$

Q2 **22·50**

£7·50 per week; £7·50 × 3 = £22·50

Q3 **17:15**

The plane lands 2 hours and 27 minutes after 14:48

So 2 hours after 14:48 is 16:48 plus another 27 minutes

which is 17:15

Q4 **0·33**

3 ÷ 9 = 0·3333… = 0·33 (2 d.p.)

Q5 **360**

Rhombus is a quadrilateral so 360°

Q6 **65**

The rule of the sequence is −5, −4, −3, −2, −1

Missing term is: 69 − 4 = 65

Q7 **5·00**

350 g ÷ 7 g = 50; 50 × 10 p = 500 p = £5·00

Q8 $\frac{1}{3}$

Months ending in 'y': January, February, May and July;

so $\frac{4}{12} = \frac{1}{3}$

Test 40

Q1 **B**

7·95 cm = radius

Diameter = 2(radius) = 2 × 7·95 cm = 15·9 cm

Q2 **C**

6 + 5 + 4 + 3 + 2 + 1 = 21

Q3 **B**

769 − 25 = 744

Q4 **E**

10% of £20 = £2; so price in Feb is £22

10% of £22 = £2·20; so price in March is £24·20

Q5 **E**

£480 = 80%; £60 = 10%; £120 = 20%

Q6 **C**

Beth: 127,700 − 127,220 = 480

Sam: 127,220 − 126,400 = 820

Emma: 127,220 − 126,999 = 221

Tom: 127,456 − 127,220 = 236

Sarah: 127,220 − 126,750 = 470

So Emma's estimate was the closest.

Q7 **C**

Double the number of people and double the amount

of time so 1 × 2 × 2 = 4

Q8 **D**

6 × 330 ml = 1,980 ml, which weighs 1,980 g = 1·98 kg

Q9 **D**

9 out of 15 shapes are quadrilaterals; $\frac{9}{15} = \frac{3}{5}$

Q10 **D**

Smallest factor of 7 is 1

Largest factor of 12,000 is 12,000

12,000 × 1 = 12,000

Test 41

Q1 **hexagon**

Figure 1 has 6 sides so it's a hexagon

Q2 **54 cm**

Each square has side length of: 36 ÷ 4 = 9 cm

Shape A has 6 of these sides; 9 cm × 6 = 54 cm

Q3 **1 km**

$\frac{4 \text{ min}}{60 \text{ min}} = \frac{1}{15}$; $\frac{1}{15} × 15$ kph = 1 km

Q4 **200 + 7A**

14 days in a fortnight; £200 for first 7 days so 7 days

left so 200 + 7A

Q5 **44**

6 × 7 = 42; 42 + 2 = 44

Q6 **72**

96 ÷ 4 = 24; 24 × 3 = 72 so 72 boys and 24 girls

Q7 **296**

200,317 − 200,021 = 296

Q8 **8**

8 + 9 = 17; 8 × 9 = 72; 8 < 9; so $G = 8$

Test 41 answers continue on next page

79

Q9 **4**
1 p, 1 p, 1 p, 1 p, 1 p
1 p, 1 p, 1 p, 2 p
1 p, 2 p, 2 p
5 p

Q10 **194**
97 × 2 = 194

Test 42

Q1 **28**

Q2 **180**
2 × 36 × 2·5 g = 180 g

Q3 $\frac{2}{3}$
4 faces of each cube are red so $\frac{4}{6} = \frac{2}{3}$

Q4 **35**
(28 × 2·5 g) ÷ 2 = 35 g

Q5 **36**
3 cubes each with 12 edges so 12 × 3 = 36

Test 43

Q1 **908**
568 g + 300 g + 40 g = 908 g

Q2 **2**
7 × 4 = 28 hours total
28 hours ÷ 14 builders = 2 hours total

Q3 $\frac{4}{7}$
4 out of 7 dogs are white so $\frac{4}{7}$

Q4 **9**

Q5 **6**
7(4) + 6Y = 4(16); 6Y = 64 − 28; 6Y = 36; Y = 6

Q6 $\frac{5}{12}$
Each cube has 6 sides so $\frac{5}{12}$ faces are painted red

Q7 **1,199**
1,843 − 644 = 1,199

Q8 **9**
134 − 70 = 64; 64 ÷ 8 = 8
So 8 minutes + 1 minute = 9 minutes

Test 44

QI **A**
0·454 < 0·455 < 0·545 < 0·555
So second largest is 0·545

Q2 **D**
22,422 + 1,891 = 24,313

Q3 **D**
2X° + 3X° + 4X° = 9X° so X° = 180° ÷ 9 = 20°

Q4 **A**
9°C − 22°C = −13°C

Q5 **C**
1 to 100 exclusive is 98 numbers
Square numbers: 4, 9, 16, 25, 36, 49, 64, 81
So $\frac{8}{98} = \frac{4}{49}$

Q6 **C**
444 m ÷ 22 = 20·181818… = 20 m (rounded to nearest metre)

Q7 **D**
745,000 × 0·0001 = 74·5

Q8 **D**
14 circles in total; 14 × 7 = 98

Q9 **B**
Number must be 5 more than a multiple of 6
53 − 5 = 48; 48 ÷ 6 = 8

Q10 **D**
Jan to Sep 2013 = 273 days; 10 light bulbs last 270 days
So 11 were needed

Test 45

Q1 $\frac{3}{10}$
3 out of 10 are black

Q2 $\frac{4}{9}$
4 out of 9 are white

Q3 $\frac{2}{5}$
8 out of 20 are striped so $\frac{2}{5}$

Q4 $\frac{1}{3}$
10 out of 30 are white so $\frac{1}{3}$

Q5 $\frac{3}{10}$
3 out of 10 are striped (Bag 1 is irrelevant)